THE CANONIZATION OF A MYTH

HEBREW UNION COLLEGE ANNUAL SUPPLEMENTS

NUMBER FIVE

The Canonization of a Myth

Portugal's "Jewish Problem" and the Assembly of Tomar 1629

Martin A. Cohen

CINCINNATI 2002

The publication of this volume
of the Hebrew Union College Annual
was subventioned by

The Henry Englander-Eli Mayer Publication Fund
established in their honor by
Esther Straus Englander and Jessie Straus Mayer

The Hebrew Union College Annual
thanks the Maurice Amado Foundation for its generous support of
this publication and its commitment to strengthening research
and education in the field of Sephardic Studies

LIBRARY OF CONGRESS CATALOGING-IN-PUBLICATION DATA

Cohen, Martin A.
The canonization of a myth: Portugal's "Jewish problem"
and the Assembly of Tomar 1629 / Martin A. Cohen.
p. cm. — (Hebrew Union College annual. Supplements; no. 5)
Includes bibliographical references.

ISBN 0-87820-604-3 (alk. paper)

1. Arquivo Nacional da Torre do Tombo (Portugal). Manuscript. Câdice
1508. 2. Councils and synods — Portugal — Tomar — History — 17th
century. 3. Jewish Christians — Portugal — History — 17th century.
4. Marranos — Portugal — History — 17th century. I. Title. II. Series.

BX1557.T66C64 2003
946.9'004924–DC21   2002192165

Design and composition by Kelby and Teresa Bowers
Printed in the United States of America

Dedicated to Professor Ellis Rivkin

Teacher, Mentor, Friend
Trailblazer in the sociopolitical analysis
of self-serving documents.

Submissions

We welcome for consideration scholarly essays in Jewish and Cognate Studies, Ancient and Modern: Bible, Rabbinics, Language and Literature, History, Philosophy, Religion. Please address offerings to, The Editor, *Hebrew Union College Annual*, 3101 Clifton Avenue, Cincinnati, Ohio 45220.

Authors submitting manuscripts for publication are asked to do the following:

1 For manuscript formatting, follow *The University of Chicago Manual of Style* in general and *The SBL Handbook of Style* specifically.
2 All manuscripts, including notes, should be continuously paginated, double-spaced and employ generous margins all around. Notes should be placed after the main text, not at the bottom of the page.
3 Every manuscript must be accompanied by an English abstract of 200 words maximum. An electronic copy will be required if the manuscript is accepted for publication.

Previous Volumes

The *Annual* office can supply vols. XLV–LXXII: vol. XLV at $10.00, vols. XLVI–LII at $15.00, vols. LIII–LVIII at $20.00, vol. LIX–LXXI at $30.00, and vol. LXXII at $40.00. Offprints of single articles, including a cumulative index for the first 53 volumes, are selectively available while the supply lasts. The American Jewish Periodicals Center at HUC-JIR, 3101 Clifton Avenue, Cincinnati, Ohio 45220 can supply microfilm copies of vols. XXXVIII–XLIV. University Microfilms, Inc., 300 North Zeeb Road, Ann Arbor, Michigan 48106 can supply 16 mm, 35 mm, 105 mm microfiche, as well as photocopies.

Supplements

Yosef Hayim Yerushalmi. *The Lisbon Massacre of 1506 and the Royal Image in the Shebet Yehudah.* 1976.

Mark E. Cohen. *Sumerian Hymnology: the* Eršemma. 1981.

William C. Gwaltney, Jr. *The Pennsylvania Old Assyrian Texts.* 1982.

Kenneth R. Stow. *"The 1007 Anonymous" and Papal Sovereignty. Jewish Perceptions of the Papacy and Papal Policy in the High Middle Ages.* 1985.

Contents

Introduction

Knowledge of a variety of documents is requisite for an understanding of the Spanish and Portuguese "New Christians," a term used primarily to designate the converts from Judaism to Christianity in late medieval Iberia and applied, at least theoretically, to all of their descendants. Of these documents certainly the most important are the trial records of the Inquisition. Their extant numbers are so large that to have read them all is far beyond the capacity of any individual. The most devoted student of inquisitional cases in our generation, the lamented Israel Salvator Révah, claimed that he had personally perused a thousand such dossiers. This represents only a minuscule fraction of the inquisitional dossiers that are housed in archives around the world. The national archive of Portugal, the Arquivo Nacional da Torre do Tombo in Lisbon, contains some forty thousand dossiers, and equivalently impressive collections are to be found in the rich archives of Spain and Mexico. Other dossiers are to be found in various public archives and private collections, largely in Europe and the Americas. The vast majority of these cases remain in manuscript. Only a small number of cases have been published, among them the dossiers of the Inquisition of Ciudad Real, in an admirable edition by Professor Haim Beinart.

But the inquisitional trial records represent only a fraction of all the primary documents necessary for an understanding of the complex beings that the New Christians were. No less indispensable are the hundreds of official papers from Church and State, dozens of polemical tracts and references in works of theology and history, and, not least, the belles-lettres of the inquisitional period, including those created by New Christians in Iberian territories and by former New Christians, now openly living as Jews, who had found refuge outside the sphere of Spanish and Portuguese control.

Ideally, all these works should be studied for an adequate reconstruction of what may best be called the "Marrano phenomenon," that is, the life of the New Christians, all of whom were subject to being regarded as Judaizers, whether they were in fact Judaizers or not.

Yet no less important than the accumulation of new data from hitherto unstudied or insufficiently studied resources is the need to reevaluate the already available and regularly repeated data in the light of new questions and new techniques suggested by contemporary scholarship.

The present study seeks to contribute in a small way to both needs. It is based on the study of a critical document hitherto largely unfamiliar to the world of scholarship. The two main chapters of this study focus respectively on a synopsis of the contents of this lengthy text and its analysis against the backdrop of its time and place. The spatial confines of the *Supplement Series of the Hebrew Union College Annual* for which it was prepared preclude the inclusion of either the document or a full translation, each of which would in itself be of book length. It would be desirable if both could some day be published. The same limitations have made it necessary to keep the notes highly selective. Especially regrettable is the necessary omission of considerable corroborating evidence from the other manuscript documents found, like the subject of this study, in the Arquivo Nacional da Torre do Tombo and other inquisitional collections. References to material directly quoted from the manuscript as well as indications of key sources are made as needed in the text proper. A fuller treatment of the pertinent literature will be found in my forthcoming works, including *The Marrano Myth: The Inquisition's Weapon Against Modernity*, now in preparation.

In this study the word "Marrano" is omitted prior to the analysis in chapter three. The reason is that the word is loaded with affect and misunderstanding. It carries with it the assumption of the secret practice of Judaism, an assumption which we clearly know was frequently unfounded. It also carries with it certain pejorative or meliorative connotations, depending on which side of the issue of secret Judaism a writer or speaker may be ranged. Instead of the term "Marrano" the more neutral and accurate term "New Christian" is used.

Heartfelt thanks are due to the may people who facilitated the preparation of this study: to Dr. José Pereira da Costa, director of the Arquivo Nacional da Torre do Tombo, and his staff, whose help in situ and through correspondence has been unflagging; to Dr. Herbert C. Zafren, Director of Libraries, Hebrew Union College-Jewish Institute of Religion when this study was begun and to his most gracious successor, Dr. David J. Gilner; to Dr. Philip E. Miller, Librarian and Ms. Amy W. Helfman, Deputy Librarian of the New York School of the Hebrew Union College-Jewish Institute of Religion, and the staff of the libraries of the Hebrew Union College-Jewish Institute of Religion, for their friendship and their continual and devoted help; to Dr. Gary P. Zola, Director of the American Jewish Archives and Ms. Eleanor Lawhorn and Mr. Philip Reekers of its staff for their alacritous help at all times; to the staff of the New York Public Library, Research Division, for its consistent courtesy, understanding, and helpfulness; to my revered teacher, Dr. Sheldon H. Blank, of blessed memory, then Editor of the Hebrew Union College Annual, when this project was begun, to his successor in this position, Dr. Herbert H. Paper, and to the present editor of the Annual, Dr. Edward A. Goldman and its associate editor, Dr. Richard S. Sarason, for their constant help in encouraging the manuscript of this work toward publication; to Ms. Donna Simmons and Ms. Edith Shayeson, for their diligent and expert preparation of the original manuscript; to my students, Rabbi Richard Prass, and rabbis-soon-to-be Mollie Cantor and Shoshana Nyer, for their help in the computerization of the manuscript; and, by no means last, to my wife, Professor Shelby R. Cohen, for her constant encouragement and invaluable suggestions.

The Background

A unique assembly convened at the Convent of Christ in the city of Tomar, some hundred and fifteen kilometers northeast of Lisbon in the spring and early summer of 1629. In was called an assembly (*junta*) and not a council (*concílio*) because it had not received the papal permission for the higher designation. It had been conceived some four years earlier by the Bishop of Coimbra, João Manuel, who guided it to actualization. The assembly was composed of some twenty ecclesiastical dignitaries and professors of theology and canon law from the Universities of Coimbra and Evora. The prelates and professors had originally been authorized to convene in Elvas, in southeastern Portugal, near the Spanish frontier. But complaints about the remoteness of Elvas had led to a transfer of venue to the more centrally located Tomar.

All of Portugal's bishops had been invited, but a number did not attend. Some, like the bishops of Miranda and Porto, sent regrets on account of illness. The Archbishop of Lisbon, who also served as Governor of Portugal, took refuge in his obligations. The Archbishop of Braga, the primate of the Iberian Peninsula, stayed home out of pique. He felt that his rank entitled him rather than the Bishop of Coimbra to leadership of the assembly.[1]

The mission of the Assembly of Tomar was to ponder a solution to Portugal's "Jewish problem," which, according to many, had gotten completely out of hand. The Portuguese Jewish problem was somewhat anomalous in that Jews had not been permitted to reside in Portugal since 1497, when its large Jewish community was converted by force and fiat. Portugal's "Jewish problem" derived from the descendants of these converts, or, as they were called *conversos*, or New Christians. The New Christians, or, as they were often also called, the "People of the [Hebrew] Nation," were collectively suspected of harboring Jewish beliefs and engaging in Jewish religious practices. Since they were canonically Christian, and were, or at least were presumed to have been baptized, such aberrant religious behavior was nothing short of heresy. The apparent diffusion

---

1 Arquivo Nacional da Torre do Tombo (ANTT), Códice 1326. See also João Lúcio d'Azevedo, *História dos christãos novos portugueses* (Lisbon: Livraria Clássica Editora de A.M. Teixeira, 1921; repr. Lisbon: Livraria Clássica Editora, A.M. Teixeira Filhos, 1975) 193–96. On the Jewish community that flourished in Tomar prior to the decree of expulsion in 1496 and the forced conversions beginning in 1497, see J.M. Santos Simões, *Tomar e a sua judaria* (Tomar: Museu Luso-Hebraico, 1943) with an introduction by María José Ferro Tavares, i-xvii, and the pamphlet, published with the Hebrew title *Bet Ha-Knesset Shel Tomar*, but with an English text and the title *Synagogue of Tomar*. This little pamphlet, valuable especially for its record of Jewish tombstones from other parts of medieval Portugal, was prepared for the group or commission for the preservation of the synagogue of Tomar as the home for the Luso-Hebraic Museum. It lacks the name of an author as well as the date and place of publication.

of this heresy in the late sixteenth and early seventeenth centuries caused more than a modicum of consternation in many circles of Portugese society.[2]

The startling aspect of the "Jewish problem" was its irrepressibility. The Inquisition, the chief organ dedicated to its eradication, appeared impotent in the face of its continual resurgence. The Inquisition arrested its suspects under terrorizing conditions. It frequently held them in its prisons for months or years before proceeding with their trials. It accepted uncorroborated testimony against them, even from interested and untrustworthy sources. It resorted to torture to extract information. It did not scruple to send to the stake as *diminutos*, that is, uncooperative, or, more precisely, insufficient testifiers, all those who in its estimation had not implicated enough relatives and acquaintances in their heretical activities. And it confiscated part or all the possessions of its convicts, even if they were reconciled to the Church. Yet, for all this, the Inquisition could neither crush the New Christians' Judaizing nor intimidate its practitioners. No sooner did it appear to be moving toward the successful repression of their heresy than it sprang up again, weedy and defiant.

That the New Christians opposed the introduction of the Inquisition and then, when this battle was lost, sought to delimit its authority at every turn was understandable. But the chronic inclination of the Papacy to support the New Christians was not. Regarded as unconscionable, it was usually explained as a manifestation of Rome's lust for money and the pandering complaisance of New Christian wealth.

New Christian money was suspected at the root of all blows to the Portugese Inquisition. These included the refusal by Frei Diogo da Silva, Portugal's first Inquisitor General (1531), to assume his office; the short-lived Pardons granted to the New Christians in 1531, 1535, 1548, and 1605; the equally short-lived suspension of the Inquisition in 1544; the ten year moratoria on the confiscation of

---

2 See Azevedo, *Cristãos Novos*, 67–111. Azevedo's work is highly biased against the New Christians. Cecil Roth's *A History of the Marranos*, with a corrective introduction by Herman Prins. Salomon (Philadelphia: Jewish Publication Society of America, 1932; repr. New York: Jewish Publication Society of America, 1974) removes Azevedo's objectionable barbs but essentially retains the slant of his thinking. See especially Roth's chap. 3, 60–61. Azevedo's work contains reference to a number of documents dealing with the background of the Assembly and found in Código 1507 of the ANTT. Azevedo does not make full use of this material. In this study the use of much of this material, v.g., the letter of April 18, 1629, on fol. 116, is precluded by spatial considerations.

The terms *converso* and "New Christian" are technically applicable as well to the Moslem converts and their descendants. These were also called the *moriscos*. In practice, however, unless clearly indicated by the context, the terms apply to converts of Jewish descent and their descendants. The *moriscos* were expelled in 1609–14. On the *moriscos*, see Henry Charles Lea, *The Moriscos of Spain: Their Conversion and Expulsion* (Philadelphia: Lea Brothers, 1901; repr. New York: Greenwood Press, 1968); Antonio Domínguez Ortiz and Bernard Vincent, *Historia de los moriscos* (Madrid: Revista de Occidente, 1978) and Mercedes García Arenal, *Inquisición y moriscos: Los procesos del tribunal de Cuenca* (Madrid: Siglo Veintiuno Editores, 1978) esp. chaps. 2 and 3.

New Christian property declared in 1558 and again in 1577; and the repeated lifting of restrictions against emigration by New Christians, especially in connection with their General Pardon by the king at Madrid in 1605.

In the years immediately preceding the Assembly of Tomar, the New Christians had again been heavily agitating for concessions. They pressed the Crown not only for a new general pardon, but also for a drastic overhaul of inquisitional procedures. The Inquisition, they said, should bring suspects to trial quickly and thereby put an end to the suicides, false confessions, and false denunciations by prisoners despairing of their unresolved incarcerations. It should reject uncorroborated or untrustworthy testimony. It should test the credibility of witnesses by repeating their depositions after an interval of time without allowing them access to their original record. It should severely punish witnesses testifying falsely against accused Judaizers. It should not condemn people as *diminutos*. It should, above all, follow the milder procedures of the Inquisition in Castile. At the same time, the New Christians demanded an end to the obstruction of their entree to public offices and honors. Such entree, they reminded the authorities, had been vouchsafed in Christian tradition and classically reiterated for them by Pope Nicholas V (1447–55) to King John of Castile (1406–54). They also pointed to the fallowness of the New Christians' useful talents resulting from their specious exclusion from societal normalcy on nothing more than a suspicion of their religious nonconformity.

As always in their petitions, the New Christians denied the allegations of their collective connection to Jewish practices and beliefs. On the contrary, they pointed with pride to the signs of their Catholic loyalty: their contributions to Catholic causes, their endowment of Catholic shrines, the entry of their daughters into convents, and even the pious cries to Jesus and Mary of many New Christians on their own way to the stake.

They even went so far as to inculpate the Inquisition for the survival of Judaizing in Portugal. Such inculpation had by now become almost de rigeur for the New Christian defense. In this connection the New Christians proposed specific changes designed to eradicate Judaism once and for all. Six such proposals were particularly noteworthy. The New Christians suggested periodic inspections of the Inquisition by representatives of the Papacy unbeholden to the Iberian crown in order to insure the fairness of the proceedings; meting out harsh punishment to all people convicted of heresy, even to the point of "relaxing them to the secular arm," which meant death at the stake (!), and including in their number all parents convicted of indoctrinating their children into Judaism; granting New Christians a perpetual "Edict of Grace," which in effect meant a standing opportunity for them voluntarily to confess their heresies, but this time with a guarantee that such confessions would not be followed by the confiscation of their property; granting New Christians permission to sell their possessions and emigrate freely; making New Christians fully eligible for public positions and honors; and ordering a limited expulsion of New Christians. The expulsion would include those who had been reconciled to the Church or had abjured the heresy of which they had been strongly suspect, that is, those who had, in the terminology of the Inquisition, abjured *de vehementi*. The New Christians also urged the removal of racial impediments to the marriages with Old Christians of New Christians who were otherwise eligible.

The New Christians expressed the conviction that, with the implementation of these suggestions, all Judaizing would disappear. The New Christians would then become completely assimilated into the general population.[3]

The New Christians' advocacy of these changes aroused bitter opposition in Portugal.[4] This opposition was hardly diminished when, shortly after the accession of Felipe IV of Spain (Filipe III in Portugal) to the throne in 1621, they offered to lend him the much needed sum of a hundred and fifty thousand ducats in return for his favor of their claim. The offer threw the young king into a quandary.

Felipe's initial response was unfavorable to the New Christians. In 1623 he ordered their representatives to leave his court, and in 1624 he instructed his governors and the Inquisition to study means for the definitive eradication of heresy from his domain. But soon thereafter, the royal confessor, Frei Antonio de Sotomayor, began to persuade the king to change his mind in favor of the New Christians' pretensions. The king hedged. In an official letter dated June 26, 1627, he tried to give something to both sides of the controversy. On the one hand he prohibited New Christians, on penalty of being regarded as teachers of Judaism, from traveling to the Indies, or requesting papal briefs in their favor and he established exile as the basic punishment for offenders reconciled to the Church. On the other hand, he authorized a three-month period of grace for New Christians residing in Portugal and six months for those overseas in its colonies. He rescinded the prohibition against emigration by New Christians from Portugal and the liquidation of their assets, but laid down the condition that those who left for lands where the Catholic religion was not permitted could not return without specific royal approval. Perhaps most important, he

---

3 For an exposition of these arguments see ANTT Códice. 1506, fols. 176–96a: "Tratado com que se pretende provar que se não deue fazer distinção de Christãos novos et christãos velhos no provimento dos Benefícios, officios e dignidades" (ms.) and fols. 232–48a, "Petição dos Christãos Novos onde pidem remedio con apontamento pera não serem differencias dos xpãos velhos ne [sic] cargos nem serem tantos presos si [sic] sambenidatos" (printed).

4 ANTT Códice. 1618, fols. 146–49, "Peitição que derão os homens de Nação hebrea do Reino de Portugal a sua Magestade no anno de 1621" (ms). See also fols. 239–53, "Sobre o perdão geral que os Judaizantes de Portugal pedem." See also Elkan Nathan Adler, "Les Marranes d'Espagne et de Portugal sous Philippe IV," *Revue des Études Juives* 49 (1904) document I, 55–58. The document, undated, is probably contemporary with these events.

declared all New Christians in whose family there had been no suspicion in matters of faith for three generations to have full rights in employment and honors. Less than two months later, in letters patent dated August 4, the king absolved New Christians who confessed their heresy during the period of grace from the confiscation of their property.

In a royal decree dated March 11, 1628, Felipe made further concessions to the New Christians. He ordered that parents teaching Judaism to their offspring should no longer be convicted as "dogmatists" without royal approval; that the penalty of exile should not be applied to children below the age of twenty; that the Portugese Inquisition should follow the practices of its Spanish counterpart; and that, in general, the inquisitional regulations should be more flexibly interpreted. Above all, he gave the New Christians and Old Christians complete freedom to intermarry, except in those cases where the Old Christian party required special royal permission to wed.

Relatively few New Christians took advantage of the period of grace to confess their sins. Their opponents seized this fact to argue their lack of contrition and to encourage greater repression.

The bishops of Portugal and the Inquisitors pressured the crown to desist from putting into effect any part of its decree, except the Edict of Grace. The Edict of Grace was a document publicly proclaimed in all places where a new tribunal of the Inquisition was established. It invited anyone among the residents of that community who might have engaged in a heretical act in the past to come forward with a confession, with the promise that the confessor would be treated compassionately. The Inquisitors took especial exception to the expulsion of penanced convicts on two grounds: that it would obstruct their investigative machinery and, further, that it was contrary to canon law, which pardoned the sin of the confessor. The Inquisition proceeded to hold one major auto-da-fé in 1628 and three in 1629, with a total of nearly seven hundred and fifty convicts.[5]

In the meantime, the preparations for the Assembly of Tomar were completed. The Assembly convened on May 23, 1629, and concluded its deliberations two and a half months later, on August 6. No record of their deliberations has come down to us. Possibly no record was ever made. But we do have a treatise drawn up by the learned doctors of faith from the Universities of Evora and Coimbra that meticulously analyzes the problem of the New Christians and advances specific and detailed suggestion for its solution. This treatise, which we shall call the Report of the Assembly of Tomar, was evidently prepared for the king. The assembly delegated two of its number, the Archbishop of Evora and the Bishop of Elvas, to deliver the report to the monarch.[6]

5 Azevedo, *Cristãos Novos*, 184–91.
6 Azevedo, *Cristãos Novos*, 194–95.

The Report of the Assembly of Tomar is one of the most important documents in the history of the inquisitional period in Portugal. It is a unique document since no such ecclesiastical assembly dedicated to the "Jewish question" had ever before been convened, nor, as things turned out, was any other subsequently gathered. Beyond this, it is a critical document for understanding the "Jewish problem" in Portugal. In its own day, as we can now see with retrospective clarity, it marked an important, even if at the time only mildly perceptible, turning point in the history of the New Christians of Portugal. In our day, its well-known point of view, presented with unmistakable clarity, lends support to the calls for a reappraisal of the entire New Christian problem.

The text of the Report has therefore long deserved a detailed description and analysis. Composed in Portugese, it is a lengthy document whose only exant manuscript runs 137 folios. The manuscript is housed in the Arquivo Nacional da Torre do Tombo in Lisbon.[7] Its contents have never been analyzed and have merited only a brief description in João Lúcio d'Azevedo's *História dos Chistãos-Novos Portugueses*. Aside from a two-page extract in Azevedo's work, no part of it has ever been published.[8]

The authorship of the text is unknown. The Portuguese bibliographer, Diogo Barbosa Machado, ascribes the authorship to one of the signatories, João de Carvalho, of the faculty of Laws at the University of Coimbra and a member of Coimbra's Inquisitional Tribunal. Of João de Carvalho, Barbosa Machado says that "he was consulted on how 'the people of the Hebrew nation' (i.e., the New Christians) could be eliminated in Portugal, to which question he answered with a learned treatise offered to Filipe III (of Portugal, who, as has been noted, was Felipe IV of Spain), which won him the veneration and applause of the most illustrious scholars." Yet there is no additional evidence to suggest that João de Carvalho played a dominant role in the formation of the manuscript.[9]

By the same token, the Spanish bibliographer, Pascual de Gayangos, lists another of the signatories, Frei Leão de Santo Tomás, as the author.[10] Frei Leão's name appears near the bottom of the first of the two columns of signatories to the document. But as in the case of João de Carvalho, there is no evidence suggesting a principal role for him. Another name hitherto not mentioned but worthy of at least equivalent consideration is that of Frey António Taveira, the last signatory on the left column. Accompanying Frey António's name is the title

7 ANTT Cód. 1508. References to all quotations in part two of this study are taken from this manuscript and are enclosed in brackets in the body of the text.

8 The excerpt is printed in Azevedo, *Cristãos Novos*, 473–74 (app. 16).

9 Diogo Barbosa Machado, *Bibliotheca Lusitana* (4 vols.; Lisbon: António Isidoro da Fonseca, 1741–
59) 2:624.

10 Pascual de Gayangos, *Catalogue of the Manuscripts in the Spanish Language in the British Museum*
(4 vols.; London: British Museum, Department of Manuscripts, 1875–93) 3:347.

"Overseer (Revedor) of the Holy Office, and Examiner of the Three Military Orders, and Prior of the Monastery of Our Lady of Light." The claim on behalf of Frey António derives from the fact that a decade earlier he had served as the Prior of the Convent of Christ of Tomar, and had published a Sermon on the Faith (Sermão da Fé) in conjunction with a visit by the Holy Office on January 1, 1619. This sermon demonstrates the same meticulous learning and the same argumentation later found in the Report.[11] Yet even in the case of Frey António it is difficult to establish a basis for authorship, especially for the entire manuscript.

Rather than work of a single author, the manuscript suggests consensus and composite authorship. Yet the entire Report meticulously follows a carefully conceived pattern and only exceptionally betrays a flaw in coordination. The manuscript is the work of at least four different scribes, the last of whom (109a–137a) is the clearest and the neatest. Elsewhere in the manuscript there are numerous cross-outs of words or entire lines of text (v.g. ff. 19a, 35a, 36a, 38a, 38b, 39b, 70a, 84a, 94a, 94b, 95b, 104a, 104b, 105a), usually accompanied by interlinear or marginal corrections; the covering of several lines by a pasted overlay of blank paper (v.g. 21a), or, more often, paper containing a correction (v.g. 24b, 33b, 42b, 96a, 101a, 102a), or cross-outs of marginal notes, with or without corrections (v.g. 89a, 89b, 91a, 91b, 106b); and one case of a major marginal addition to the text (67b).

It is impossible to know whether more than one copy of the text was originally prepared, or whether multiple copies circulated at any time. Two Spanish translations of the Report are extant, both in manuscript. One of these, housed in the British Museum, contains 139 folios;[12] the other, of 192 folios, is found in the Ets Haim Library in Amsterdam.[13] Neither the date of the translations nor the identity of the translators is known. It is not unreasonable to conjecture that the translations were intended to disseminate the Report in the larger Spanish-speaking section of the Iberian empire. If so, they would have carried official sanction.

The translations, while very close, are not identical. There are different spellings of the same word, translations of the same verb by different tenses, different translations, and different marginal glosses. There are even instances (v.g. the dates in BM 126a and EH 96a) where neither manuscript follows the original.

11 *Sermão da Fé* ... Lisbon, por Pedro Craesbeeck, Anno 1619. See esp. fols. 3a ff. and 25a, "Pello que ... heregia." Likewise incorrect is its statement to the effect that "the treatise had to be *written* in Spanish because of the Spanish domination of Portugal, which lasted until 1640" (emphasis added). That both Spanish versions are translations there can be no doubt.

12 British Library, *Additional Manuscript*, 28462.

13 Ets Hayyim HS, EH 48 d 26. For a description of the manuscript, see Lajb Fuks and R. G. Fuks-Mansfield, *Hebrew and Judaic Manuscripts in Amsterdam Public Collections* (2 vols.; Leiden: Brill, 1973–75) 2:212.

The analysis of the texts of the translations lies beyond the scope of this study. Such an analysis might go far toward answering the question of the possible existence of multiple manuscripts of the original.

The calligraphy of both manuscripts is good, but the manuscript of the Ets Haim is the more beautiful, largely because a generous number of its titles and other parts of the work are artistically lettered.

The Report is divided into eight parts. These fall naturally into three categories: An analysis of the New Christian problem past and present (parts I–III): an analysis of the diffusion of Judaism and the complaints of the New Christians (parts IV–VI); and a consideration of the various alternative solutions to the "Jewish problem," the recommendation of a specific course of action, and suggestions for its appropriate implementation (parts VII–VIII). The material in the first of these categories was in all probability prepared in advance of the Assembly. Certain sections or a complete rough draft may also have been prepared in advance for the second and third categories, but their final form had to be shaped by the three and a half months of deliberation at Tomar.

The Report reveals a stunning range of erudition. Its material is derived from more than two hundred different sources and is reflected in nearly a thousand individual citations, exclusive of the Bible, whose official Latin translation, the Vulgate, is itself cited over two hundred times. Though there are marginal references for nearly all the sources utilized, these are, as is the case with many premodern manuscripts, often incomplete. Frequently only the author is cited. This is particularly frustrating when the author was prolific, like Augustine or Aquinas. When the title of the work is given, the citation is usually not further identified. In addition to their reliance on well-known works, these references also reveal contact with sources that are now difficult to retrieve. These are cited simply as "papers," "Laws," "rules," "edict," "royal decree," "Letter of Philip II," "Letter of Cardinal," or, in one instance, "Book dealing with Criminals."

The citations from the Bible include approximately one hundred thirty from the Vulgate's Old Testament and the New Testament. The prophets, especially Isaiah, dominate the citations from the Old Testament, while most of the New Testament references are to the Gospels and Acts of the Apostles. Every subsequent period of Christian tradition is represented, from the Church Fathers to the early seventeenth century. So is every important genre.

In biblical exegesis, the Report relies heavily on Jerome's commentaries (late 4th and early 5th centuries [henceforth only the number of the century of major activity will be given]) and utilizes others, like those of Basil (2), Philo of Carpasia (4) (cited as Philo Carpathius), Ambrose (4), Procopius Gaseus (6), Theophylactus of Ochryda (11), Abbot Rupert of Deutz (12), Hugh (Cardinal) of Saint-Cher (13), Nicholas de Lyra (14), Alonso Tostado (15), Jerome Oleaster (Gerónimo Oleastro) (16), Juan Maldonado (16), Pietro Colonna Galatino (Galatin)(16), Tommaso (baptized Giacomo) de Vio Gaetani (Cajetan)(16), Francisco de Toledo (16), Juan de Pineda (17), and especially the *Brevis explicatio sensus literalis totius Scripturae ex optimis quibusque auctoribus per epitomen collecta,* an as-yet unprinted work by Giovanni Stefano Menochio (1575–1655). The work was to be published in Cologne in 1630.

In the area of church law, the Report cites the encyclopedic works of Ulpianus (Ulpian)(3); Justinian's code (6) and its famous commentary, that of Bartolo of Sassoferrato (14); the *Dictionarium Juris* of Alberic of Rosate (14); the *Commentaria in Decretales* by Peter of Ancharano (15) and the work of identical title by Philipe de Dexio (16); the *Práctica civil, crimnal y canónica* of Juan Gutiérrez (17); the *Conclusiones omnium probationum ac questionum quae in utroque foro quotidie versantur* of Giuseppe Mascardi (16); the *Commentarium Juris Civilis in Hispaniae Regias Constitutiones* of Alfonso de Acevedo (16); the *Suma de la teología moral y canónica* of Enrique de Villalobos (17); and extensively, various works of two renowned Italian jurisconsults, Jacobo Menocchio (16) and Prospero Farinacci (17). To this list should be added the canons of various Church councils, especially the Iberian councils held at Toledo during the Visigothic period and related works like the *Discourse* pronounced in the Council of Trent by Gaspar del Fosso Ricciulo and published at Louvain in 1567.

In theology, primary attention is, of course, given to the works of Thomas Aquinas. The Report also cites important theological works of Gregory of Nazianzus (4), Cyril of Alexandria (5), Isadore of Pelusium (5), Prosper of Aquitaine (5), Pope Gregory I (6), Paschasius Radbertus (9), Bruno the Carthusian (11), Hugh of St. Victor (12), Bernard of Clairvaux (12), Vincent of Beauvais (13), Augustine of Ancona (14), Angelo Carletti de Chivasso (15), Cajetan (Tommasio de Vio)(16), Nicholás Alfonso de Bobadilla (16), Claude Togniel d'Espence (16), Juan Blas Navarro (16), Pedro de Ribadeneyra (16), Mateo Salcedo (16), Luis de Molina (16), Juan Márquez (17), Francisco Suárez (17), and Atanasio García (17). To these should be generically added the sermons of men like Cyprian of Carthage (3), Peter Chrysologus (5), Pope Leo I (5), and Abbot Guerric of Igny (12).

Among the apologies for Christianity and Church, including attacks against a variety of heresies, the Report cites writings of Theophilus of Antioch (2); Origen (3); Lactantius (4); Arnobius the Elder (4); Eusebius (4); Gregory of Nazianzus (4); Theodoret of Cyr (5); Augustine (5); Fulgentius of Ruspe (6); Germanus I, Patriarch of Constantinople (8); Nicephorus, Patriarch of Constantinople (9), Alfonso de Castro (16); Alfonso Salmerón (16), Enrique de Villalobos (17) and Robert Cardinal Bellarmine (17).

Of works directed primarily against the Jews, the Report utilizes the writings of Justin Martyr(2), Tertullian(3), Epiphanius(4), John Chrysostom(4), Isidore of Seville (6), Julian of Toledo (7), Anastasius Sinaita (7), Agobard of Lyons (9), the fictitious "Letter of Rabbi Samuel" attributed to Samuel of Morocco (11), who is claimed to have converted to Christianity; Peter Damian (11), Andronicus of Constantinople (12), Vincent Ferrer (15), the former Jew, Pablo de Santa María (Pablo de Burgos) (Solomon Halevi) (15), Bernardine of Siena (15), the former Jew Gerónimo de Santa Fe (Joshua Lorki) (15), Alfonso de Spina (15), Peter Galatin (16), and Amador Arráez (16).

In the field of history, the Report relies on the *Historia Ecclesiastica* of Eusebius (4), which also cites Hegesippus (2); the *Historia Francorum* of Remigius of Reims (6); the *De Origine Actibusque Getarum* of Cassiodorus (6); the *Historia Ecclesiastica Gentis Anglorum* of the Venerable Bede (8); the *Byzantina Historia: Graece et Latine* of Nicephorus Gregoras (14); the history of the Popes (*Liber de Vita Christi ac Omnium Pontificum*) of Bartolomeo Platina (15), the *Memorabilium Omnis Aetatis et Omnius Gentium Chronici Commentarii* of Johann Naucleus (16); the *De Rebus Gestis Francorum* of Paulus Emilius (16), the very influential *Anglica Historia* of Polydore Vergil (16), the *Ecclesiastica Historia, sive Metropolis, De Primis Christianae Religionis in Saxonia initijis* by Albertus Kerantius (Krantz) (16); the *Ilustraciones genealógicas de los Reyes de España y de los Emperadores de Constantinopla hasta el rey don Felipe II y sus hijos* of Esteban de Garibay y Zamalloa (16); the *Cronología Universal* of Jerónimo Martel y Losilla (17), the *Crónica universal de todas las naciones y tiempos* of Alfonso Maldonado (17) and, above all, the *Annales Ecclesiastici* of Caesar Baronius (16).

The Report naturally also cites a number of works directly connected with the Inquisition. These include the *Directorium Inquisitorum* of Nicholas Eymeric (14), the *In Directorium Inquisitorum Nicholai Eymerici Commentaria* of Francisco de Peña (16), the *De Origine et Progressu Officii Sanctae Inquisitionis* of Luis de Páramo (16), the *Tractatus de Sancto Inquisitionis Officio et Ejus Utilitate* of Domingo de Mendoza (16) and the *Orden que comúnmente se guarda en el Santo Oficio de la Inquisición acerca del proceso en las causas que en él se tratan* of Pablo García (17). In addition, considerable use is made of the *Defensio Statuti Toletani* of Diego de Simancas (16), published under the pseudonym Didacus (Diego) Velázquez.

The Report also occasionally cites the work of Renaissance humanists, including Marsilio Ficino (15), Lúcio Marineo Sículo (16), Juan Luis Vives (16) and Benito Arias Montano (16).

In addition, the Report reveals a broad knowledge of the Greek and Roman classics. It cites Plato's *Laws*, Aristotle's *Nicomachean Ethics* and *On the Heavens*, Strabo's *Geography*, Caesar's *Gallic Wars*, Tacitus' *Annals*, Valerius Maximus's *Factorum ac dictarum memorabilium* and, among the Jewish writers in Greek, Philo's *On the Special Laws* and *On Creation*, and Josephus' *Antiquities*.

Noteworthy by their absence from the Report are Jewish sources, aside, of course, from the Vulgate's Old Testament, Philo and Josephus, and the writings of former Jews like Pablo de Santa María and Gerónimo de Santa Fe. At least since the middle of the thirteenth century, rabbinic materials had been used by Christians for their anti-Jewish polemics. Such materials are found in Pablo Christiani's polemic at the Disputation of Barcelona (1263), Raymund Marti's *Pugio Fidei*, Pablo de Santa María's *Scrutinium Scripturarum*, Gerónimo de Santa Fe's *Hebraeomastix*, and others. A little more than a decade after the composition of the Report of the Assembly of Tomar, António Machado was writing his *Espelho dos Cristãos Novos*, with a respectable amount of rabbinic material.

Yet the absence of rabbinic materials is not difficult to explain. The Report is not primarily a polemical text, nor is it primarily concerned with the theological motifs, such as the question of whether the Messiah has arrived, which preoccupied Christian-Jewish polemics in the Iberian Peninsula. It is rather an analysis of the "Jewish question" from two vantage points: contemporary practicality and *Christian* tradition.

To appreciate its importance for a comprehension of the "Jewish problem" in Portugal, we turn first to an analytical resume of the Report and then to an analysis of its significance.

The Report

THE STRUCTURE OF THE MYTH

The first section of the Report lends itself to a tripartite division. The first part intends to demonstrate the depravity of the Jews, the second the *conversos'* deleterious influence on Christianity in their newly-acquired faith, and the third the baneful effect of the New Christians in Portugal. The first division derives its arguments almost entirely from Scripture and Christian tradition, the second from Christian theology and history, and the third from the history of the Portuguese *conversos*.

The fundamental motif in this section of the Report is psychological rather than logical. While the Report does not eschew a recourse to fact and syllogism, it generally and in this section normatively places greater emphasis on affective appeal and emotional conviction. The pillars of its argument are presented fragmentarily and are laced together with suggestion and innuendo. Its frequent repetitions are hardly fortuitous. They are all variations on its major themes, their different settings and nuances serving to drive home their cardinal thoughts with visceral impact.

To demonstrate the evil inherent in Jews of all ages, the first part moves chronologically from pre-Christian times through each of the first sixteen Christian centuries, citing examples from the Old and New Testaments and leading spokesmen of the Church. Its reliance on sacred tradition is motivated by the quest for indisputable authority. "There can be no better or surer proof to establish any proposition," it says, "than the infallible truth of Scripture and the testimony and judgment of such qualified people," and further, "We must believe that the Holy Spirit attends and governs them with special providence" [3b–4a].

The demonstration is achieved by saturating the text with citations from these authorities, usually in Latin, along with the Doctors' translations, paraphrases and commentaries. The nucleus of each citation consists of at least one adjectival or nominal referent to a specific Jewish flaw or vice. Repeatedly the Jews are described as foolish, ignorant, senseless, errant, ungrateful, envious, impudent, evil, iniquitous, malicious, provocative, perverse, perfidious, disobedient, disloyal, rebellious, lawless, fickle, and inconstant. But most frequently by far they are characterized as incredulous, unfaithful, obstinate, insensitive (or hardhearted), deaf, and especially blind. In the twenty-one folios constituting this section, Jews are associated with blindness forty-four times, insensitivity and deafness forty-three, obstinacy thirty-four (including stubbornness [10] and contumaciousness [6]) and faithlessness and incredulity twenty-four.

Interwoven with these descriptions are the Doctors' repeated assertions that the Jewish condition is irremediable and incurable because the Jews are inherently unrepentant and incorrigible. In this connection they cite, among other things, Ambrose's opinion that the Jews are more obstinate than the Devil [9b]; Isidore of Seville's view that the Hebrew people are as impervious to change as blacks to whitening or animals to altering their traits or colors [14a]; and Aquinas' reminder that it is to the Jews, inferentially of all times, that Isaiah addresses the epithets "princes of Sodom" and "people of Gomorrah" [19a]. The Doctors go so far as to emphasize that the religious infidelities of Jews exceed those of idolatrous Gentiles. With Luis Vives who, ironically, as we now know, was of Jewish descent, they go so far as to say: "It is easier to convince any of the pagans who do not as defiantly contradict the truth than to dispute with such obstinate and perverse people" [23a]. And to cover the future, they cite Gregory of Nazianzus' cry of despair to the Jews: "I do not believe that you will ever hear me out or be persuaded . . . even if you should live the years of Methusaleh on earth" [11a].

These considerations lay the groundwork for the principal theme of this segment, namely, that the evil qualities of the Jews have manifested themselves no less than in other areas, in their approach to the Christian faith. Some fifteen passages in this section attest to the Jews' stubborn insistence that "We have no king but Caesar" [22b] and their obstinate refusal to accept Jesus and all the miracles, especially the Virgin birth, connected with his arrival. This rejection is regarded as nothing more than a continuation of the Jews' inveterate opposition to God, which the Report harps on in carefully planted excerpts from the authorities. Since God and Christ are identical, it follows that the Jews have always been opposed to Christ. The Jews are thus enemies of Christ and God. Because they refused to receive Christ, they are the equivalent of the anti-Christ, the Doctors say with Agobard, or devils, according to Hegesippus. The Report reiterates the fable of a pact between the Jews and the Devil. Beyond mere refusal to accept Christ, the Doctors say, the Jews bear an innate hatred to Christ, the Virgin and all Christians. They even took the life of Christ, in fulfillment of biblical predictions. To illustrate the extent of this hatred, the Doctors record the comment by the eleventh century sage Theophylactus of Ochryda on Mark 15:27: "and they crucified two robbers with him, one on the right and one on the left." Theophylactus explains that "by the robbers are meant the Hebrew people and the pagans. But the pagans are equal to the good thief. He was grateful and recovered his senses. The Jewish people is equal to the wicked thief. He blasphemed Christ to the end" [26a–b].

The Jews' refusal to accept the miracles of Christianity, the Doctors tell us, has continued throughout history. In the fourteenth century, for example, Saint Nicephrous of Constantinople miraculously healed a cripple by immersing him in baptismal waters. Many pagans and Greeks converted, but the miracle had no effect on the Jews.

The reprehensibility of such obstinacy and blindness toward Christianity is dramatically illustrated by the dream of the real or imaginary Jew, Herban, with whom Gregory engaged in a polemic. In the dream, Herban sees Moses speaking with Jesus and adoring him. Herban asks Moses whether it was good to adore Jesus, to which Moses, in contradiction to his own obstinacy and that of his people, stated that he recognized in Jesus "my maker and lord" [11b].

For their execrable attitudes and behavior, the Report declares that the Jews are deserving of condign punishment. They have, in fact, already been severely punished. They lost their prophets and sages, Jerusalem was destroyed, and Jesus' blessing continues to remain concealed from them. Incurably blind to begin with, their punishment thus paradoxically consisted in their consignment to perpetual blindness. In support of this thinking, the Doctors call upon Peter Damian: "The very light of the Incarnation which filled the temple of the Virgin with brightness and beauty, blinded the understanding of the Jews" [16a]. And Eusebius: "Because once the Jewish people dared to commit that monstrous crime against Christ, darkness, ice and cold formed over them. Because their minds were benighted to such a degree, the light of the Gospel was unable to send rays into their hearts" [9a]. And Aquinas, explaining Revelation 8:7 ("And the first trumpet sounded and there came hail and fire, mixed with blood . . ."): "The preaching of the Gospels to the Jews was turned into hail, fire and blood because of their opposition, as a result of which they deserve to remain in the same blindness in which they were before" [19b].

The Jews' handicap in faith was foreshadowed by Jacob's wrestling with the angel, the angel representing the Word Incarnate and Jacob the Hebrew people which was "left forever lame in faith"[12b]. A similar expression is found in Cardinal Cajetan's comment to Matthew 21:19, where Jesus, "seeing a lone thick tree by the road, came to it and found nothing on it except leaves. Jesus cursed the tree saying, 'No longer shall there ever be any fruit from you.' And at once the fig tree withered." Cardinal Cajetan saw in the fig tree a representation of the Hebrew people: "Because he [Jesus] could not find in it the holy fruit of inner faith and virtues but only of ceremonies and external rituals he cursed it forever . . . and it immediately withered into eternal barrenness" [21b].

The Jews, the Report insists, are therefore sterile in faith. They are like a lone voice in the desert or spiritual wanderers in the wasteland. This was biblically prefigured, according to Procopius Gaseus, by Hagar, the "mother of the Jews" (!) and the incarnation of the synagogue, who was cast out of Abraham's house. Her rejection, says Procopius, "is equivalent to degeneration and removal from faith and religion. She immediately was lost and remained in the desert wandering and astray" [13a]. Comparably, Pope Leo I, commenting on Matt 27:45, which tells of the darkness that fell on the land from the sixth to the ninth hour of Jesus' agony, explains that this meant that the Jews were to be forever deprived of the light of the inspiration of grace and the sanctification of all the sacraments [12a–b].

The text emphasizes that this rejection is perpetual. "Never will the breach with God be healed" [22b]. Because the Jews abandoned God when He became a man they will forever be abandoned by God. Like Ishmael, who according to Andronicus of Constantinople represents the Jews, they have been "ejected from the house of God and condemned *to the end of the world*" (emphasis added) [20a], or as Philo Carpathius says, "a veil is imposed on their hearts: certainly they still feed on its lethal shadow to *eternal death*" (emphasis added) [10a]. The Doctors add that the prophecy of Psalm 68:23[14] has been fulfilled on the Jews: "Let their table become a snare and a trap, and a stumbling block and a retribution to them. Let their eyes be darkened and see not and bend their backs forever" [7a].

The obvious conclusion of all this is that the Jews cannot possibly be saved "because they lack the faith of Christ" [15a], a lack which, of course, is irremediable. They are thus benighted, accursed and abandoned forever. Cyril of Alexandria finds an allusion to this irrefragable reality in John 18:8 in the falling back of the Roman cohort and the officers of the priests and the Pharisees after Jesus' revelation. This, he says, is "a symbol of the fall of the Jewish people of the future" [12a]. The Doctors say with Jerome that "until today the wound of Israel is not cured by the medicine of supplication nor bathed with oil that their hardness might be softened by the tears of repentance" [10a], and with Vives that the proof of the Jews' blindness, deafness, and obstinacy lies in the lengthy continuation of the punishment which God has always meted out to them for their denial and crucifixion of Christ [22b–23a]; and with the *converso* Gerónimo de Santa Fe that "the Jews' refusal to acknowledge Christ's arrival and to accept him as the Messiah is born of the hatred which they have always harbored towards him; and for this reason they have suffered the endless captivity which they are in" [21a]. The Jews, the body of the Report reminds us, are "destined for captivity, and this captivity has continued among the Jews throughout the world until today. It is recognizable by the obloquy and scorn in which the Jewish people lives in the midst of the nations" [14b–15a].

The concentration on their accursedness responds to the practical goal of isolating the Jews as reprobates "with spirits obstinate in Judaism" [22a]. The Report points out that the prophets who foresaw the Crucifixion — by the Jews — could also foretell that future Jews would "want to be like heirs and participants in as great an iniquity as the death of Christ" [9a]. The Jews' traditional enterprise with respect to Christianity, it emphasizes, "has been to curse and blaspheme until this very day" [24a]. It records an incident in Paris when a Bible covered with choice cloth was presented by the Jews to Pope Innocent III, at which time Innocent reminded the Jews of their infidelity and blindness. He also prayed for

---

14 In the Vulgate. In the Hebrew Bible it is 69:23.

God to lift the veil that prevented them from seeing and knowing Christ [17a].

Innocent's hope, of course, was vain, since, as the Report emphasizes, the Jews, by nature, are eternally resistant to conversion. Because they stubbornly persist in infidelity, they will not be saved. The Scriptural and traditional sources allowing for the conversion of Jews before the end of time do so only for a limited few. This is the meaning of Jeremiah 3:14: "I will take from you one of a city and two of a family and I will bring you to Zion." By Zion, says Galatin, Jeremiah means salvation. Galatin finds another foreshadowing of the exceptional salvation of individual Jews in Numbers 13 and 14, where of all the multitudes of Jews, only two individuals, Joshua and Caleb, entered the Holy Land [22a].

While this part of the Report manifestly deals with Jews, occasional statements suggest the continuation of Jewish propensities among contemporary converts and descendants of converts from Judaism. Thus the reference to feigning and dissimulation among contemporary Jews could not have failed to be susceptible to application to the New Christians by the average Portuguese in the seventeenth century. A reference by Chrysostom seems directed to *conversos*: "they in fact violate the temple of the Lord by a conscience inclined to Judaism" [10b], while Cajetan's judgment that "this people was worse after it abandoned Christ than before, amidst its idolatries" [21b], unmistakably refers to recidivist *conversos* rather than unconverted Jews.

If few such statements appear in this part of the Report, they nevertheless signal its obvious goal: to demonstrate a connection between the New Christians of seventeenth century Portugal and Jews of all ages past.

Not directly linked to the major theme are a number of hostile and incendiary remarks. One blames the Jews for founding heretical sects, among them the Essenes! Another disparagingly refers to the alleged messiah Bar Kokhba, whom it perhaps intentionally calls Barcochina, since the word *cochino* means "pig," and whom it equally erroneously regards as having reigned for thirty years. A third charges Jews with falsifying Scripture, especially through what it calls the "fables" of the Talmud, which is described as a "new law containing many precepts opposed to the old Law given by God to Moses" [15b]. A fourth is Pope Leo's comment on Matt 27:51–52 referring to the death of Christ: "The rocks were split and the tombs were opened." Pope Leo says that these words intimate the Jews' impiety, which is harder than rocks. In the Passion of Christ, Leo says, the Roman soldiers were mild compared to the Jewish priests, because the soldiers repentantly beat their chests in contrition while the priests insulted Jesus on the cross [12b]. And hardly escapable from the reader familiar with the Iberian world of the Inquisition are two other quotations of Biblical prophecy, one from Jeremiah (11:16), the other from Ezekiel (5:1), both affirming that punishment for at least some of the Jews is to be brought by fire [5b, 15a].

In these discussions, the Doctors also cite the indictment of Jews by their former coreligionist, Pablo de Santa María, author of the *Scrutinium Scripturarum*,[15] "of the same blood and race ... therefore great attention should be paid to his testimony" [20b], and the fictitious "Letter of Rabbi Samuel," allegedly written by a convert from Judaism whom the letter claims to be the late eleventh century Rabbi Samuel of Fez.[16]

The next division in this section of the Report deals exclusively with converts from Judaism. Its purpose is to demonstrate the undiluted persistence of Jewish belief and practice among all converts and their descendants regardless of their apparent piety. The frequency of allusions to the depravity of the Hebrews decreases in this division; yet attention sufficient for reinforcement continues to be drawn to their errors, corruption, insolence, disobedience, rebellious-ness, deceit, superstition, obstinacy, pertinacity, and above all, their dissimula-tion. Of such characteristics three appear with greatest frequency: the falsity, faithlessness, and retrogression of the New Christians. The chord struck from the very beginning is that no sooner throughout history did the Jews convert to Christianity than "they returned to their vomit ..." (2 Peter 2:22) [25b, 26b] and that "they are so unsteady, fickle and inconstant in the faith they received, that God Incarnate himself did not trust such a fragile Christianity" [24b]. All signs to the contrary notwithstanding, Jewish converts to Christianity — and again, all *conversos* are intended — are "false, evil, and feigning Christians" [27a]. "None of them truly professes the Law of Christ nor does any of them convert sincerely," they say, quoting Alonso Tostado, "rather they convert only to live honorably and with a measure of respect among Christians, but they do not lose the memory of the Law [of Moses] in which they were reared" [26b]. They are inveterate enemies of the Church, the Doctors affirm. They breed heresies within it and in general try their hardest to destroy it.

The second and third parts of the first section become progressively more historical. Both give examples of apostasy by new converts from Judaism result-ing from their inherent Jewish depravity. The second part focuses primarily on Castile and Aragon while the third concentrates on post-1497 Portugal.

The second division cites twenty specific historical instances of what it re-gards as cases of egregious backsliding by converts from Judaism as well as unconverted Jews, who are regarded as racially identical with them. The list is prefaced by a noteworthy reference to the sin of the golden calf. The Doctors clearly regard the Hebrews' retrogression immediately after the Sinaitic covenant as a prolepsis of their future retrogression as New Christians.

15 See Luciano Serrano, *Los conversos D. Pablo de Santa María y D. Alfonso de Cartagena* (Madrid: C. Bermejo, 1942).

16 See Arthur Lukyn Williams, *Adversus Judaeos* (Cambridge, England: Cambridge Univ. Press, 1935) 228–32.

To accomplish this major theme, the Doctors cite perfidies by converts and unconverted Jews. In Visigothic Iberia Jewish converts to Christianity invited Jewish merchants from North Africa in 684 to the hurt of the entire land. In Zaragoza in 1487, the New Christians plotted to kill the Inquisitor of Aragon [33a].[17] In other parts of Europe, Jews were expelled for "very grave offenses against the Christians" [31a], including the poisoning of wells in France in 1320 and 1348, which also resulted in popular riots against them [31b–32a]. Similarly, the Report attributes the anti-Jewish violence in Castile and Aragon in 1391 to the alleged poisoning of wells by Jews two years earlier [32a–b]. These riots revealed the recidivism of the Jewish converts to Christianity, say the Doctors. They reason as follows: The Visigoth monarchs compelled all Jews to leave Iberia or convert. All who remained therefore accepted Christianity. Since all subsequent Jews [sic] in the Peninsula descended from them [sic] they therefore were also New Christians. Consequently, the large number of Jews victimized in 1391 could only be *conversos* who had "returned to the errors which they carried stamped on their souls" [32b].

The Doctors find further evidence of this phenomenon in the exiles of 1492. Among them, they claim, were many New Christians who chose to leave the Peninsula in order to live elsewhere as Jews. This unexpected information raises a question: Were the Doctors referring to New Christians descended from Jews converting in the years beginning with the riots of 1391, or to Spanish Jews, who, through the Doctors' own understanding of history, could only have been descendants of the converts remaining in the country as a result of the Visigoths' ultimatum?

As it develops its evidence for the innate recidivism of the Jewish converts to Christianity, the Report affirms that their conversions were insincere and motivated by the desire to save their lives and property. The converts could not wait to return to Judaism at the first possible moment, says the Report. In the meantime they organized synagogues, circumcised their sons, taught Judaism to their children and, in general, flouted the proprieties of Christianity. So powerful was their urge to Judaism, the Report insists, that it infected "pure" Christians and resulted in a spread of Judaism, especially in Iberia. In each case, therefore, it became necessary for popes, Church councils, and kings to seek remedies for their "Jewish" problem.

These remedies took various forms: In some instances, the Jews or converts were forbidden to reside among other citizens, have contact with them or offer testimony against them. They were prohibited from serving as physicians, "because of the little faith of these people and the risk incurred by anyone who puts himself into their hands, given the hatred they bear for us . . . [28a]. They were barred from positions of trust and honor, secular as well as religious. These

---

17 The reference is to Pedro Arbués, Inquisitor in the tribunal of Zaragoza.

included positions in the royal household and exchequer and appointments as notaries. The Report justifies such exclusions on the grounds that "since all Jews [in the racial sense of the term] possess depraved customs and are cloaked with envy and hatred, with which they persecute Christ, never forgetting the evils they inherited from their ancestors, it is not just or proper for the Republic to admit to such offices those who have made themselves unworthy through their own or their ancestors' vices" [28a–b]. The remedy most frequently mentioned is the expulsion of all the Jews in a given territory. Although all such instances involved unconverted Jews, the Report understands the words "all Jews" to include as well the converts from Judaism and their descendants, whether they identified as Jews or, as far as could be told, lived like good Christians.

Spiced with the emotive epithets of blindness, impiety, and perversity applied to the New Christians, the Report reviews the history of Portugal in the years 1492 to 1628 in such a way as to hold the New Christians responsible for all the ills that befell the country.

The basic contours of this history are well known. In 1492 the indigenous Jewish community of Portugal was increased approximately tenfold by an influx of refugees from Spain who had chosen the alternative of leaving their homeland as Jews over the opportunity of remaining there as converts to Christianity. The Portuguese king, João II (1481–95), against the advice of many of his nobles, admitted a few of these Jews to residence and granted most of them an eight-month stay, in return for a sizable payment. King João really wanted them to remain in Portugal because he needed their skills to develop his domestic economy and the funds they could generate for his military campaigns. But, for a variety of reasons, he wanted them fully integrated into Portuguese society as Christians. He therefore spared no efforts to induce their conversion to Christianity. He compelled them to listen to proselytizing preachers. He took their young children from them, to be reared as Christians, and announced to their parents that they would not see them again unless they converted. But, except for rare instances, he failed time and again to secure the Jews' corporate conversion. His successor, Manuel I (1495–1521), continued these efforts, but also met with failure. Manuel found himself on the horns of a dilemma when the Catholic Sovereigns of Spain demanded that he rid himself of the Jews as a condition for their acquiescence to his desired marriage with their daughter. Reluctantly, he issued a decree of expulsion in December, 1496, but continued his efforts to convert them. When everything else failed, he herded as many Jews as possible into the buildings in Lisbon known as Os Estãos, subjected them to a variety of indignities, and finally dragged them to the churches for baptism. The baptismal waters did not touch all the Jews, but all were nevertheless declared to be Christians.

Once this violence was over, Manuel sought to integrate these new Christians fully into Portuguese society. He returned their children, declared a twenty-year moratorium on inquiries into the orthodoxy of the converts, and sought to eliminate all distinctions between New Christians and Old. Because large numbers of New Christians left Portugal in the next two years, Manuel, in April, 1499, closed the borders to their further emigration. In 1515, Manuel secretly inquired about the possibility of establishing an Inquisition on the Spanish model in Portugal. His successor, João III (1521–57), proceeded vigorously to work for its introduction. Despite powerful opposition from the New Christians, the Inquisition was established in 1536, and despite further efforts to limit it, it was given most of the power it desired in 1547.

The Report reduces the history of the Jews under João II to a single paragraph. It admits the violence against the Jews, but attributes such acts as the seizure of the children to the "zeal and piety of some" [34a]. And it attributes the conversions of the Jews between 1492 and 1497 to the desire on the part of Jews to avoid the disasters that befell their coreligionists at sea.

Manuel, it goes on to say, wished to make amends for the injuries to the Jews. He declared them free from their official slavery and rejected a sum of money with which they wished to express their gratitude "because the zeal which he had for the Christian faith inclined him to attract them to the bosom of the Church with kindness and humaneness" [34a]. His seizure of the Jewish children was motivated by pity for their innocence, the Report says. It does not implicate the king in the violent conversions of the Jews, but emphasizes that the Jews "received baptism only as a means to preserve their physical life" [34b]. As a result, the Doctors argue, "the mysteries of the Church were daily profaned by the New Christians" and "the sacraments which Christ ordained in it at the cost of his precious blood were unworthily received"— because, they say, "like criminals who never departed from their incredulity and [their original] faith, they managed to obtain the restoration of their children and a twenty-year moratorium against investigation for errors of Judaism" [34b]. They not only remained steadfastly Jewish, but they even corrupted venerable Old Christians, including priests. They had synagogues and rabbis, and even a false Messiah. Many left the country to live openly as Jews in Holland [sic!] and other foreign countries, especially Italy, taking Christian servants along with them for conversion. The evils they occasioned in Portugal impelled João III to request an Inquisition like Castile's. The "Jews" opposed this with their power and impeded the steps to its establishment by receiving pardons and exemptions from the confiscation of their property, only to Judaize the more, even when in Inquisitional confinement, this despite their remonstrances in their request for pardon that they were Christians. They denounced the Inquisitor General Cardinal

Henry and his staff as cruel enemies and prejudiced judges. With such false words, they persuaded the Pope to grant them special favors and privileges. The Pope even determined to send a papal nuncio to inspect the Inquisition. This resulted in greater embarrassment for the Church since the New Christians boasted that the nuncio had been bought with their money.

Even worse, such privileges enabled them to corrupt many Old Christians with money to testify on their behalf. They even dared to murder a fellow New Christian, Henrique Nunes, known as Firme-Fé [Firm (in) Faith],[18] for revealing their heresies to the king.

Only the determined efforts of the king led to the establishment of the Inquisition in 1547. Yet even the Inquisition had failed to resolve the "Jewish problem" in Portugal. The number of New Christian Judaizers had actually grown so phenomenally that "those who have fled the country have filled the other kingdoms while those who have remained are so bold and rich . . . and they have become so brazen in their apostasies that they have not committed them furtively or denied them in their petitions" [37a]. Furthermore, the New Christians are "so inconstant and unfaithful that thirty, forty, or fifty years after their conversion they said that their baptism had been effected with violence and intimidation. And they designated as forced Christians [Hebrew: *anusim*] not only the converts who chose to remain in the kingdom during all this time (though they could have left it); they even applied the same to their children and grandchildren" [37a–b]. These people, the Report declares, are "hard and stubborn: their penalties, punishments, and pardons have done them little good" [37b].

In Portugal the New Christians filled the Inquisition's jails. They bought a pardon from King Sebastian (1557–78) with a large sum of money, not for the opportunity to become good Christians again [sic!], but "to return with full vigor to their Judaism" [37a–b]. After the pardon, these people were just as Jewish as before. Cardinal Henry had opposed the pardon, urging the king not to permit the delinquency of these people and their perversion of others. Other influential people protested that it was unjust for the king to condemn his would-be assassins while he pardoned the perpetrators of divine lese majesty.

The effect was quick in coming. The king's agreement with the New Christians "opened the door wider for their practice of Judaism and provoked divine punishment of the same kind that God had so frequently used to visit this kingdom" [38a]. This time the Portuguese armies sent to fight the Muslims in North Africa were disastrously routed and King Sebastian was killed.

18 See Alexandre Herculano e Araujo, *História da origem e estabelecimento da Inquisição em Portugal* (3 vols.; Lisbon: Imprensa Nacional, 1854–59), translated by John C. Branner as *History of the Origin and Establishment of the Inquisition in Portugal* (Stanford, Calif.: The University, 1926) and reprinted with an erudite prologomenon by Yosef Hayim Yerushalmi (New York: KTAV, 1972) 286–87.

The New Christians' intrepidity continued during the reign of Felipe III (of Spain, who simultaneously ruled in Portugal as Filipe II [1598–1621]). They requested the removal of all distinctions between Old and New Christians and as well a general pardon. They finally received the pardon during the early years of the reign of Felipe IV (of Spain [1621–65], who simultaneously ruled in Portugal as Filipe III [1621–40]).

With this pardon, the New Christians came out of the Inquisitional jails but remained as Jewish as ever. Many left the Peninsula, publicly embraced Judaism elsewhere and then returned to Portugal "to vomit up the poison they had drunk in the synagogues of Italy," and, the Doctors add, "there was no one to accuse them" [38b]. These abuses finally provoked a royal order prohibiting discussion of the New Christians' request that prisoners' possessions should not be confiscated. Portugal once again was punished: many of those involved in granting this pardon suffered disastrous ends, as did nearly all the ships and the cargo which the money was used to buy.

With the abrogation of the pardon, the population of the Inquisitional jails increased; yet the New Christians' pressure for favors have continued well into the reign of Felipe IV. But, the Doctors declare, "we trust in God who directs and governs the hearts of kings that since his Majesty is so pious and Catholic and the greatest defender of the Church, he will never[19] admit their proposals which in the name of clemency and remedy are really intended against the Christian religion and the purity of faith" [39a–b].

The Report recapitulates: "In sum we shall say only that in all these years . . . Portugal has witnessed stupendous sacrileges and all other crimes which this [Hebrew] nation committed in the most ancient times in various parts of the world after the cruel death they inflicted on the son of God" [39b]. Among other things, the New Christians stole ciboria with consecrated hosts; they defiled the images of Christ and the Virgin Mary; they established synagogues and Jewish associations at home and abroad; they vitiated the divine mysteries and profaned the sacraments, and did other things which terrified the faithful. Some of these have been publicly disclosed while others are kept secret in the archives of the Inquisition. The Report concludes that the New Christians "are most perverse in their customs, as is evidenced by their usuries and other greater transgressions with which they defame the Portuguese nation — the concealed deaths of the sick contrived by their pharmacists and physicians; the secret contacts, associations, and relationships with the enemies of this crown and the monarchy of Spain, and the schemes they offer them, since it is certain that

19 At this point the original text has the following words crossed out: "give ear to these stratagems because they are all" and then goes on to the word "intended." My translation is based on a marginal note substituting for these words. The Spanish translation does the same.

they are the reason why other nations sailed to the Indies, and went to Brazil, disturbing the conquests achieved with so much blood" [40a].

This division concludes with a brief coda intended to demonstrate the vain efforts by the kings of Portugal beginning with the mass conversions to win their converts to sincere Christianity by "paternal love." "To their own prejudice," the Report says of the monarchs, "they showered them with favors, including positions at court, the privileges of the nobility, important knighthoods, the military orders, the hierarchy of the Church and the most honored posts in the government and legal structure of the Republic." They also "encouraged their marriages with people of noble blood and performed many other favors for them" [40b].

Such acts, the Report goes on to say, only disheartened the monarchs' "native subjects" and "gave them occasion to complain against these people." The result has been "our great shame and confusion" [40b]. This, it goes on to say, justifies the exclusion of the New Christians from offices and honors "which should be conferred only on upright persons . . . clean and loyal" [42a].

This leads the Doctors of Tomar to the first unequivocal statement of their solution to their "Jewish problem," as they ask the king to expel all New Christians "from this kingdom and all its conquered territories." Recognizing that this request could not anticipate immediate implementation, they suggest a compromise. "At least," they urge, "none of them should be permitted to learn Latin or study science, or be admitted to high offices of the Republic, the Exchequer or the Bench, or hold any other positions which could be prejudicial to the public good, and that the laws which render them ineligible to serve in high positions be fully and unexceptionally enforced, and that no contract of the kingdom pass through their hands, since it is patent and notorious that the entire profit remains with these contractors, and that they alone become powerful with the large profits they reap . . ." [42b].

It will become evident that the practical solution the Doctors had in mind involved a combination of these two alternatives: the expulsion of some alleged New Christian Judaizers and the retention of others in Portugal under surveillance and control.

THE JUSTIFICATION OF THE MYTH

That the Doctors of Tomar did not expect their drastic proposal to find easy acceptance is evident from the efforts they expended in its justification. They recognized that the attainment of their goal would depend in no small measure upon their success in confronting three formidable obstacles: the aversion in both natural and canon law to the imposition of collective guilt; the New Christians' powerful objections to the procedures of the Inquisition; and, among important segments of the Portuguese elite, the widespread disinclination to regard Portugal's "Jewish Problem" as one of critical proportions. It is therefore to the demolition of these obstacles that the three major considerations of the central section of the Report are devoted.

On the question of collective guilt, the Doctors cite the New Christians' position, buttressed by natural law, civil law, and Christian tradition, which holds that "everyone about whom there is doubt is deemed to be good and innocent" [44b]. The New Christians insisted that the charge of heresy, "the most serious of all transgressions," collectively imposed upon them was unfounded. On the strength of favorable sources, they pointed out that heresy, though born of the mind and understanding, is discernable only through expression in perceptible words and actions, and that indictments of any kind are improper in the absence of such expressions. "On the contrary," they argue, "it would appear prejudicial to presume so ill of an entire nation and community and to affirm that all its members are false and feigning though they live as if they were Christians" [45a]. It would be just as unfair for people to be deprived of rights or positions because they belong to such a community.

Furthermore, they plead that philosophers agree on the impossibility of upholding a generic charge. Generic charges tend to be vague and rounded by imagination. In the area of faith, they allege, "it appears impossible to corroborate a suspicion against an entire nation unless everyone of its members is shown to be estranged from it" [45a].

In contradiction, the Report argues as follows: Certain characteristics are regarded as inherent in entire nations. In this regard, the Doctors quote Jerome's judgement that the Greeks are fickle, the Moors vain, and the Jews stiff-necked. Individuals are influenced by the group: example becomes custom and custom turns to ingrained habit. Philosophers like Plato attribute these processes to stars, atmosphere and environment and deduce virtues and vices for an entire people from them. Theologians attribute such characteristics to human communication and interaction. In fact, when the crew of the ship carrying the stowaway prophet Jonah asked to what nation he belonged, it was, they say, for the purpose of determining his characteristics [46a].

For the same reason, the protagonist in Tobit (5:10) asked the angel who appeared in the guise of a young man to accompany his son, from what house and tribe he came. "Even for such a position," the Doctors say, citing the Venerable Bede, "it was necessary to descend from virtuous ancestors in order for the son to be entrusted to him confidently and without fear" [46b].

The law frequently recognizes generic attributions, particularly of vices which, according to Aristotle, take root more easily in a group than virtues.

But even more important than ordinary communication is "the communication of blood and its transmission from parents to children" [46b]. This was recognized by the Bible, where God commanded the Jews not to marry foreigners on the supposition that idolatry might adhere to them and their progeny through such unions. So certain is the communication of vices from parents to children that both imperial and canonical laws *restrict and occasionally punish the children of felons* [46b].

Individuals not guilty of the vices attributed to an entire community may yet be regarded as delinquent, just as an entire body is regarded as sick if its principal parts are ailing. The Bible itself frequently characterizes the entire people Israel as foolish, disloyal, useless and entirely removed from God despite the fact that it was clear that Israel "possessed all the wisdom that there was in the world and so many worthies and saints that the twelve thousand from each tribe whom St. John says that he saw in his apocalypse [Rev 7:4–8] was merely intended to give us a general idea with this limited number" [47a].

Furthermore, the argument that every Christian should a priori be regarded as observant crumbles in the face of sufficient presumption to the contrary. The presumption is most natural in the case of religious offenses, which are more readily communicated than others, especially from parents to children. This makes it possible to judge on what otherwise might appear to be limited evidence that an entire nation may profess a faith externally yet harbor infidelity in its heart.

The presumption of individual innocence is not applicable to heretics, who are known to dissemble in matters of faith, however piously Christian they appear. With heresy, the presumption of individual guilt is acceptable to the degree that an entire community or nation is involved in the charge leveled against the individual. As for the deprivation of the rights of an individual, a distinction should be drawn between the receipt of Christian sacraments and being a faithful Christian. The Church offers sacraments to everyone.

The Doctors also insist that groups or classes of people constitute realities, thereby denying the nominalist position of the philosophers that a class is not a reality and that a name given to it is only a generic label.

The Doctors enumerate twelve psychological and historical details which together create the clear presumption of the New Christians' collective guilt:

1. Their natural obstinacy and refractoriness toward God.

2. Their innate tendency to religious retrogression.

3. Their violent baptism in Portugal, which made them reject their new faith from the beginning. It led to their dissimulation in its regard and the transmission of their rejection to their children. Their hostility even affected the descendants of voluntary converts.

4. Their wicked perseverance in their many errors from the time of their baptism and their cloak of Christian piety, which have even deceived Church leaders.

5. Their wickedness, manifest in their repeated petitions for general pardons, accompanied by offers of considerable money. This betrays their flaunting of Judaism between pardons.

6. The increasing intensity and hubris of their Judaizing, which makes them recidivist heretics, worthy of summary consignment to the flames.

7. The history of papal and royal expulsion of the Jews for being "unworthy of living among Christians" [54a] because of their perfidy, and the similar unworthiness of the New Christians, who regard themselves as Jews.

8. Despite their baptism and dispersion throughout Portugal, the New Christians' insistence on keeping apart from other Christians and living like a separate nation with their own inner government "through heads of families and tribes" [54a]; and their working as a unit in petitioning favors and providing purses for their members prosecuted by the Inquisition.

9. In addition to the New Christians' own identification as Jews, their notorious reputation as such abroad, with the result that all Portuguese abroad are regarded as Jews.

The Doctors feel compelled to mention two frequent objections to this allegation: first, the apparent presence of many true Christians among the New Christians, and second, the many examples of devout Christianity by New Christians who serve in religious fraternities, celebrate the saints, endow chapels, masses and suffrages, and in general expend their wealth in pious deeds.

The Doctors dismiss both objections categorically: If some New Christians are held in high esteem, they say, it may be that those who so hold them have no knowledge of their evil ways and judge them only by their external deeds, which they preform only because these help their secret schemes. Their pieties are specious, because "it is notorious that these very people who have spent their funds on charitable, pious and good acts have fled to foreign kingdoms where they publicly frequent the synagogues, while those arrested here confess that their conspicuous religiosity is really dedicated to their own saints and martyrs for Judaism" [55b–56a]. The blindness, blasphemies and sacrileges of the New Christians justify the repeated request for their disqualification from public office.

10. The justifiable disqualification of Jews and their descendants from ecclesiastical office and various religious institutions in the Peninsula.

11. The current corruption of the court in Madrid by New Christians who have migrated there. All New Christians are corrupt.

12. The large numbers of men and women of all ages and walks of life, among them lay and ecclesiastical scholars, priests and religious, as well as many with only a little Jewish blood, condemned by the Inquisition of both Portugal and Spain.

Unlike the worthy Eleazar (II Maccabees 6:18–31), who preferred martyrdom to the performance of the rituals of another faith, the New Christians, the Doctors explain, have always combined an internal devotion to Judaism with an external acceptance of Christian ceremonies in the belief that their Judaism was not thereby compromised.

This evidence of New Christian corruption should overcome all misplaced compassion for them, the Doctors urge, as they advocate the separation of faithful Christians from the unfaithful.

The Doctors again confront the objections to collective indictment in Aquinas and the nominalist argument in contemporary legal thinking. Aquinas insists on exempting the innocent from punishment and a clear demonstration of malice and obstinacy in the case of all others. The nominalist argument holds communities to be constructs and not realities and therefore not liable to punishment. Some who concede that communities can be punished for collective and deliberately incurred guilt deny the demonstrability of such guilt in the case of the New Christians; "It appears," they insist, "that the entire community can in no way be punished for them" [59b].

In refutation, the Report argues that princes and republics not only can proceed against entire communities but are obligated so to do [60a], both for the "natural" goal of removing the obstacles toward the ends which every republic desires and the "supernatural" goal of the republic's felicity. Although parents and children should not suffer for one another, nor the innocent for the wicked, the Report, leaning on Aquinas, points out that sometimes the apparently innocent are really guilty for failing to correct the sins of the others which they have witnessed or for setting a poor example themselves.

With Aquinas, the doctors divide punishments into two categories: criminal or vindictive punishment, to be visited upon delinquents themselves, and civil or "medicinal" punishment, intended to remedy a specific ill or attain some good. The latter punishment may be imposed upon an entire community even if the community is without prior fault or dereliction. Thus, while the criminal penalty (death at the stake) may not be applied to New Christians indiscriminately, the civil penalties of confiscation of property and exile may. Such procedure, founded on the concepts of public welfare and good government, will also serve as a deterrent for other subjects.

The Report even speaks of a social contract between a prince and his subjects to insure "the peace and felicity of the Republic" [61b]. The contract increases the prince's obligation to punish and stop heresies "because the spiritual and temporal dangers which derive from them are so much greater and because offences against the divine majesty are more serious and therefore all the more deserving of greater punishment and prevention" [61b]. The Report cites Pope

Leo's attribution of the stability of Theodosius' reign (379–95) to the Emperor's custom of expelling all heretics and schismatics.

Applying such reasoning to "this community of Hebrew people," the Report again recalls their obstinacy, pertinacity, and rampant Judaism, their secret synagogues and usuries, and the impossibility of their rehabilitation. Therefore "it is necessary," says the Report, "that your Majesty choose this remedy of proceeding against the entire community, both because of your obligation to punish the serious crimes within it and because as a Catholic prince and a good father of his people, you are obligated to seek not only what is good for the Republic, but what is best for it and what serves it best and most benefits it. In this case that is to remove once and for all the enemies of a kingdom so illustrious in the observation and preservation of the faith and free it from the danger in which it finds itself of becoming entirely corrupted by the presence of such noxious heretics" [63a]. The Report now again suggests that the king expel these enemies and confiscate their possessions.

At the same time, the Doctors evince a practical willingness to compromise. They suggest that, if not the entire community, at least "those who are fully New Christians" should be exiled and their possessions confiscated, because, they say, these people are the major source for the spread of Judaism [63a].

In support of their position, the Doctors claim that the case of the New Christians meets Aquinas' conditions of malice and obstinacy for corporate punishment, while innocent suffering is irrelevant here because a temporal rather than spiritual punishment is being suggested. Turning the tables on Aquinas, they place the burden of proof on the defenders of the New Christians' innocence. They reject the argument that a community cannot commit a crime. The New Christians act as a group, they explain. They do not rebuke one another for their crimes; rather, their powerful leadership seeks pardons and special favors on behalf of the entire group, the guilty included. "In these acts there is present a covert consent and open dissimulation of the above errors and crimes" [64b].

The Doctors report that their suggested remedy conforms entirely to the procedures of polities which corporately expelled their Jews. They cite seven examples of such expulsions and an alternative of incarceration for political offenses and nine of group expulsions or immolations for religious offences. The first group includes expulsions from: 1. Rome and Sardinia by Tiberius (19 C.E.); 2. Rome by Claudius (49–50); 3. Judea by the prefect Rufus (130); 4. Rome by Constantine ("the Great," d. 337) "because they rebelled";[20] 5. Alexandria by Bishop Cyril after another uprising (414); 6. Germany (1348) for

---

20 The historicity of this allegation is questionable. The reference may have been stimulated by Constantine's anti-Jewish legislation, particularly the severe decrees of 329 and 335.

causing a plague (The Black Plague); 7. Magdeburg (1384 and 1425) for the same reason; and 8. a commutation of expulsion to incarceration in Bohemia for abetting an enemy (date unknown).

The second group includes expulsions from 1. Aurelia (1009) for inciting the Sultan in Babylonia to destroy the temple in Jerusalem [sic]; 2. France (1198) for the practice of crucifying a Christian child on Good Friday;[21] 3. All of France (1295 [read 1306]); 4. Again from France by Philip (read Charles VI, through the regent Louis of Anjou) one hundred years later (1394), for purchasing a consecrated host; 5. Poland (year not given) by the king, who took all minor children from the Jews to raise them as Christians;[22] 6. Various German principalities (1410) for planning the ritual murder of a Christian boy. The immolations took place in 7. the German town of Fürst or Frisia in the year 1288 for the ritual murder of a monk;[23] 8. the province of Güstrow[24] and 9. Bavaria (in 1338 [read, probably, 1336–37]), for a similar crime.

The report emphasizes that these punishments were universally supported throughout Christendom and never repudiated by the Church. Similar collective punishments were slapped on colleges and universities. The popes themselves utilized this means to dissolve the Order of the Templars because a few of its members had been found guilty of wrongdoing. It was utilized as well by the seventeenth council of Toledo against the Jews who had been converted during the reign of (the Visigothic King) Sisebut (612–21). It harmonizes with the opinion of more recent church writers who hold that in a just war one may capture the innocent along with the guilty.

The Report further recalls that a number of princes and republics, such as England in 1291 [sic] and Spain in 1492, expelled the Jews not for any specific offense, but merely as a precautionary measure, in order to avert "the evident temporal as well as spiritual danger which results from their contact and perverse customs" [68a]. In Spain the Catholic Sovereigns attached greater weight to the potential damage resulting from the continued stay of these people in the country than their right of domicile and property. Similarly, in 1266, Pope Clement IV asked King Jaime of Aragon to expel the Moors from his kingdom, while the king of Naples expelled baptized Jews because there were clear signs of their apostasy.

Turning to the New Christians' objections to inquisitional procedures, which they regarded as a major obstacle to their full assimilation into Portuguese society, the Doctors go to great lengths in an attempt to demonstrate that, for all their apparent differences, the Inquisitions of Portugal and Spain are essentially alike.

21 Actually Philip Augustus expelled the Jews in 1182 and permitted them to return in 1198.
22 This incident is not verifiable.
23 Or, more likely, this refers to the Munich holocaust of 1285.
24 The date is not given.

The Portuguese Inquisition, they claim, is by no means harsher than its Spanish counterpart. The disappearance of Judaizers in Spain through absorption no more testifies to the blander nature of the Spanish Inquisition than their persistence in Portugal suggests the Portuguese Inquisition to be more severe. This persistence is rather due to the greater refractoriness and faithlessness of the New Christians in Portugal than to the greater harshness of its Inquisition. Actually, the punishment of Judaizers in the early days of the Spanish Inquisition was severe, while in Portugal the indulgent treatment of the converted Jews in the years immediately after their conversion and the subsequent general pardons facilitated the continuation of Judaism.

To demonstrate the substantial conformity of the Portuguese Inquisition to its Spanish counterpart, the Report rejects the specific complaints of the New Christians. It denies that on principle the Portuguese Inquisition creates inordinate delays in bringing prisoners to trial. Delays, it says, are caused by one or a combination of three factors: the overcrowding of court calendars resulting from the large number of arrests for heresy; the Inquisition's pious desire to favor the accused by carefully investigating the credibility of witnesses, and the opportunity it gives prisoners who stubbornly defend their innocence to make appropriate confessions and win reconciliation to the Church. It denies that the regulations of the Spanish Inquisition that are imprecise as to date, time and substance regarding the admission of testimony are in any way stricter and therefore more protective of defendants than their counterparts in Portugal. It defends the Portuguese Inquisition's rigorous adherence to the concealment of the names of witnesses from the accused, as against the occasional disclosure of such names by its Spanish counterpart, on the ground that this procedure is canonically correct and spares the witnesses from possible retaliation by the defendant's family and friends. This, the Report insists, is especially necessary in Portugal where the "people of the Nation are so rich and powerful, and their wickedness is so great" [74a].

The Report upholds the Portuguese procedure of reading the witnesses' testimony back to them for their ratification at a date subsequent to their original testimony. It claims that this procedure has the support of leading exponents of canon law and facilitates the emendation of one's original testimony. The Spanish system of taking the same testimony a second time while withholding the original transcript from a witness leads only to discrepancies, denials, and confusion, the Report maintains.

The Report provides a lengthy defense of the admissibility of uncorroborated evidence from a single witness. The need for multiple testimony is moderated, it says, when the crime is of the kind that can be committed in secret, like heresy, since a greater evidential demand would make the revelation of truth impossible. The basic court procedures are violated even more by the admission of testimony from criminals, perjurers and others usually disqualified from testimony, yet the testimony of these people is received, "because in both cases favor is given to the Faith, and reason militates against allowing such an enormous transgression to go unpunished" [76b]. The reliance on singular witnesses in cases of divine lese majesty is supported by the fact that such practice is followed in the less serious instance of human lese majesty. Besides, canon law itself admits the depositions of individuals testifying to acts at different times in cases that continue over a period of time, where their composite creates a coherent picture of the offense. Taking advantage of a requirement for multiple corroboration, a Judaizer could escape all punishment by teaching people Judaism on an individual basis. According to the legists, multiple witnesses are invalidated if their testimony differs with respect to the time, place or circumstances in the case of a non-repetitive crime like homicide. But witnesses in different places and times attesting to the repetition of the same substantive act are regarded as mutually corroborative. This principle may be applied specifically to the instance of heresy if several witnesses testify to the fact that a defendant is a heretic, but detail diverse heretical acts or statements. The fact of the heresy is accepted without further proof, even though it may not be possible to proceed against the defendant for a specific heresy. If, on the other hand, different witnesses testify to diverse acts or expressions of a specific heresy, like the practice of Islam, Calvinism, or Judaism by a Christian, the specific heresy is taken as proved. The legality of the procedure with individual witnesses is demonstrated by Rome's repeated rejection of petitions for procedural change importunately sent by the New Christians. And, the Doctors point out, these rejections come despite the fact that the New Christians are "so astute and powerful" [80a]. From all these considerations, they say, it follows that the procedures of the Portuguese Inquisition are in line with those of Spain.

The Doctors also reject the New Christians' claim that their penalties are prejudicial to their descendants. The great prejudice of the crime of heresy, they believe, consists rather "in the great losses and evils which it occasions for the Christian republic" and that "the spiritual and temporal good of all Christianity should be placed before the individual good of the criminal" [79a–b].

The Doctors conclude their argument by suggesting that the Portuguese practice on witnesses be introduced into the Italian Inquisition.

The Report supports the Inquisition's condemnation of the "*diminutos*" (those who are accused of refusing to implicate all the people they suspect of Judaizing) and suspected false witnesses. It dismisses the claim that delays in the processing of cases and unbearable conditions in the jails impel the Inquisition's prisoners to confess falsely in order to escape from their protracted incarceration and save their lives, which they might lose if they continued in the denial of their guilt. The Doctors emphasize the Inquisition's concern for its prisoners. Its officers, they say, "attend to the prisoners' cleanliness and treatment with great meticulousness whether they are healthy or sick and do so with such kindness that many of them were not as well treated in their own homes." They insist that "whatever is necessary for their comfort is not lacking," that "the prison acts only as a security for those arrested" and that it has "no greater severity than the chains and bars which they are dragging" [81b]. Furthermore, the Doctors recall, the prisoners' frequent implication of their kith and kin militates against the New Christians' arguments. If they were to denounce their enemies, they could be suspected of lying in order to leave the jail. But since they mention their own relatives, this could hardly represent false information. Besides, say the Doctors, many of the confessions are made in the first days after an arrest and not after a long incarceration.

Responding to the charge that some prisoners commit suicide in desperation over the severity of their imprisonment, the Report states that suicides testify not to the severity of the Inquisition but to the correctness of the charge of heresy leveled against the accused.

The Doctors likewise reject the claim that torture induces false confessions. Tortures in Portugal, they say, "are lighter and more sufferable than those administered by the Inquisition in Castile or practiced by secular courts" [82a]. Criminal confessions could therefore hardly be the result of fear of torture, they reason. Besides, they remind their intended readers, all depositions must be ratified in accordance with strict inquisitional regulations and must agree with the testimony of the witnesses they name. "In all of this," they insist, "the procedure is carried out with probity and truth" [82a]. Indeed, they claim, the abundant evidence from torture only confirms the spread of heresy and the number and degree of the defendants' accomplices.

The Doctors inveigh against the claim that false confessions are often made at the last moment by prisoners who are about to be executed. The Doctors uphold all such declarations, saying that "only a few find themselves in this predicament compared to many others who make long confessions" [82b] before this situation occurs.

They bestow their greatest attention on the charge "that in all the cities and villages in the kingdom of Portugal where prisons have been established by the order of the Holy Inquisition, not a single person is left even minimally related to the Jews or descended from them who has not been arrested" [83a]. The New Christians find it impossible to believe that all these people could be Jews [the term here has a religious connotation] only on the basis of having some Jewish descent, and keep their Judaism secret for such a long period of time. "Therefore, it is more likely that those who are arrested, in order to escape and leave the prison, mention the names of all people who they know are partially Jewish [the term here has a racial connotation] in their confessions" [83a]. The Doctors respond sharply that such evidence is valid and points to the extent of Judaism in Portugal affecting "even those who are only Jewish to a small degree" and that "therefore there is no doubt . . . that merely of the partial Jews many are penanced and relaxed to the secular arm." They observe that some of these Judaizers have been influenced by "*a single drop of blood* . . . to such a degree that they were burned alive" [83a] (emphasis added).

The Doctors affirm that instances of Judaizing have frequently been kept secret for a long time. Their discovery therefore shows that "human artifices are of no avail against divine judgements, which dispose matters in such a way that their faults and sins are made public despite their desire to keep them concealed" [83a–b]. The reason is simple: "The same councils and brotherhoods they have organized to communicate secretly and the houses joined in their interior to one another . . . in most of the cities and towns in the kingdom, on the one hand serve to bring them all together, but on the other, where a prisoner has desired to mitigate his situation because, having been arrested, he cannot deny his accomplices without risking his life, he reveals all who are in communication with him" [83b].

The Doctors rebut the contention that uncorroborated confessions are insufficient to convict. Such a situation rarely happens, they say. If it does, the confession is perfectly acceptable because unlike other crimes, there can be no more certain and clearer proof than an individual's confession of his own heresy! [83b].

They also reject the complaint about the admission of testimony that is vague, unspecific, or given by perjurers or co-conspirators. They state that the inquisitors are expert lawyers and interrogators; that they weigh the testimony of witnesses "in favor of the faith" [84a]; that they are practical and expert and can elicit specifics through questioning, and that, as with crimes occurring only once in the distant past, the specific date is not necessary in repetitive crimes. Furthermore, witnesses do not give such evidence in order to harm their accomplices but to clear their conscience under penalty of law.

The Report charges that the New Christians' challenges of inquisitional procedure are aimed at undermining the institution. The Doctors cite what they regard as a common occurrence: "The people of the Nation," they say, "hold those executed as heretics and apostates in such high regard that with the same obstinacy and pertinacity with which the condemned have denied the crime they have committed, they wish to canonize them as true Christians [sic]" [85a]. The New Christians, they say, insist that the evidence which led to their "relaxation" to the secular authorities was not correct and legitimate because "it is not likely for men and very weak women who die at such a time emotionally embracing the cross of Christ and invoking his name and that of the Virgin Mary with such evident signs of being Christian Catholics to have in their hearts another religion which they do not confess, while at the same time being in a position to avoid death by the mention of their faults" [85a].

The Doctors retort that the cases against such New Christians have been conclusively proved and that their last piety is specious. They again recall what they regarded to be a Talmudic precept, that Jews may keep Judaism in their hearts while externally displaying a different religion in order to deceive the simple "or at least to leave ordinary people perplexed and in doubt" [85a].

The Report curiously distinguishes between New Christians who die professing Christianity and the death of other, "true" Christian martyrs. The New Christians meet death not only with resignation, we are told, but also with joy, while true martyrs despise death. The New Christians, the Doctors propose, are in the clutches of the Devil. Their death shows the extent of the Devil's power over their hearts as well as their bodies. The Doctors quote with favor Augustine's statement that "it is not possible for people without a Christian life to die a martyr's death" [85b]. It is not the penalty but the cause that makes a martyr, the Doctors affirm. The New Christians are "martyrs of the Devil." They go to the fire "confident and fearless because of their vainglory in showing themselves unmoved and constant in their religion, in which they are dying honorably, as they think, by holding it in their hearts." They are actually "dying obstinately in their errors, and God permits this as a punishment for their pertinacity and hardness" [86a].

The Doctors proceed to confute three New Christian contentions: first, if they were truly Jews, they would teach Judaism to a wide circle of family and friends and would be exposed by them; second, to extinguish Judaism effectively in Portugal, New Christians should be permitted to marry Old Christians, something they would reject if they were really following Jewish law; and third, they have been demonstrating their sincere Christianity by endowing convents and sending their daughters there to live in poverty. The New Christians do teach Judaism to family and friends, the Doctors say. They keep their activities so secret that, when they are denounced, the denunciations do not agree in detail. Marriages of New to Old Christians only infect more descendants. Such unions provide the New Christians with greater security and enable them to maintain their Jewish family trees with "the memory of their tribes" [86b–87a]. The New Christians place their daughters in convents after they are imbued with Jewish practice in order to give them "security and confidence . . . to offend Christ and commit sacrileges in the holiest places . . ." [87a]. The recent penancing of some seventy nuns appears to provide ample proof of this, the Doctors say.

Finally, the Report turns to a demonstration of the critical nature of Portugal's "Jewish problem" through an analysis of why "this sickness has the deepest roots and therefore is almost incurable" [88a], that is, why Judaism has spread throughout Portugal. To this end, the Report records the discovery of both "intrinsic" and "extrinsic" causes.

The intrinsic causes derive from the nature of Judaism: As a vice, this heresy is more adhesive and more readily assimilated than virtue. It kindles like fire and spreads like cancer. Besides, the Jews multiply greatly as witnessed in the Bible by the Hebrews' phenomenal growth between the Exodus and their entry into the Holy Land. In Portugal, Judaism also grows through New Christian marriages with Old Christians. In such families "paternal love impels parents to instruct their children in their religious beliefs *while the inclination of blood impels children to learn and follow the errors taught them*. A New Christian can reap no [religious] benefit from communication with an Old Christian spouse as used to be the case in the early Church . . . Nor can a New Christian child attain any benefit from the teaching and example of its Catholic parents" [89a–b] (emphasis added). This explains the Church's prohibition of such marriages in reversal of its earlier policy.

The Doctors compare the Church's new stance with the refusal of the sons of the patriarch Jacob to give their sister (Dinah) in marriage to the Prince of Shechem [sic] and with God's decree that his people should not marry idolaters. In the second instance, the Jews, like the New Christians, are called the idolaters while the "non-Jews" or Old Christians are God's own people.

The Doctors offer two other explanations for the spread of Judaism. One is that "since this people is devoted exclusively to business and commerce and is not consumed by military activity or poverty and manual labor but rather always live in their luxurious and lavish houses . . . the number of these people grows more abundantly and Judaism grows with them" [89b]. The other is the appeal of the "infection" of Judaism among leading Old Christians. The nobility, the universities, and the various arms of the Church have all suffered their share of inquisitional arrests. This corruption of leadership creates a special problem in the example that it sets. The New Christians, in the meantime, are emboldened to spread their religion even more.

The final intrinsic cause is the greed or desire to possess temporal wealth inherent in Jewish tradition. This is known to theologians: they commonly hold that the Law of Moses offers no other promises than those of temporal gain. The ability to increase their wealth is regarded by New Christians as a sign of the correctness of their inward adherence to the Law of Moses in disregard of the baptism they have received. The worst thing about this situation are the people who honor and support this accumulation of wealth without realizing that eventually everyone who trusts it will be condignly requited.

The Doctors pay even greater attention to the extrinsic causes for the diffusion of Judaism. One is the "excessive favor with which we treat the people of this nation out of the greed we have for their money and wealth" [91b]. They recall the biblical account of Elisha's servant Gehazi, whose greed led to his affliction with Naaman's leprosy. The leprosy was not limited to Gehazi alone; it was transmitted to his descendants as well (!).

They point with approval to Naboth, who rejected King Ahab's money, and Abraham, who refused to touch any of the goods he had captured from the kings of Sodom, fearing the contagion of their vice. "If in the same way all of us would flee the material possessions of this people whom we regard as apostates or at least would feel how contemptible they are because of the infamy of their owners," the Doctors say, "Judaism would long ago have ceased or at most would continue only among them" (!) [92a].

Equally baneful, they believe, was the kindness shown by princes and popes to the New Christians of Portugal in the days immediately following their conversion because, they claim, it led to their excesses throughout the entire republic.

The restoration of the children who had been taken from the New Christians led to the perversion of these children. The twenty-year moratorium on the confiscation of the property of convicted Judaizers led to their full devotion to Judaism without fear of reprisal. Punishment cannot reform these people, the Doctors affirm: they know that they can avoid death with false confession and repentance. Yet only punishment can keep them in check.

Another cause is the general pardons. Once they were promulgated, Judaism spread throughout the country. The jails were emptied and the transgressions of the Judaizers could not be easily exposed.[25]

The New Christians therefore went about their business freely and openly, flouting all pious efforts to convert them to true Christianity. The favors extended to the New Christians thus changed them little if at all.

Even the severe laws intended for the extinction of Judaism have succeeded in removing only some of its poisonous branches, while its trunk remains alive and its roots remain as firmly planted as ever, the Doctors claim. The poisonous branches are individual New Christians, the trunk the New Christians as a body, and the roots — by inference — the millennial tradition of Judaism. These must be eradicated, say the Doctors, as God did when He destroyed the assembly of the wicked to its very roots, according to Ecclesiastes (8:10) [sic]. God removed the proud from their power and vanity and gave their honors and dignities to the humble and meek. "If therefore we wish completely to banish the errors of Judaism from Portugal and prevent it from growing so obviously among the Hebrew nation," the Doctors say, "let us not be content with remedies which stop on the surface. Let us rather go straight to the roots . . ." [94a].

The final cause is the failure by the Portuguese prelates to convene a national council "which is the means ordained by the Church to prevent such misfortunes" [94a]. The Doctors argue at length for such councils, citing as precedents the fourteen national councils in Visigothic Toledo in the eighty years beginning in 614,[26] most of them, they claim, for the purpose of arresting Judaism. By contrast "in the one hundred and thirty years of notorious New Christian apostasy in Portugal," including "their insolent mistreatment of sacred images and robberies

25 The reference is to the implication of others as Judaizers by prisoners of the Inquisition.
26 While there were fourteen councils held at Toledo in the eighty (actually sixty-one) years culminating in 694, only eleven of them could be called "general councils." The Councils of Toledo numbered IX (655) and XI (675) were provincial, while XIV (684) was a gathering *sui generis*.

of hosts" [95b], no such council has previously been held. The Doctors regarded such councils rather than assemblies involving secular authorities to be the appropriate vehicles for dealing with matters involving religion.

In the final section of this division, the Doctors turn to an exposure of the New Christians' implacable hatred of all "true" Christians. To the New Christians they attribute entirely "the storms and shipwrecks to which this kingdom is subjected, in which not only one but many Judases and apostates are found" [96a]. They invidiously distinguish between the New Christians and the "native Portuguese," although they admit that the New Christians are themselves natives of Portugal and of long Portuguese descent. They point out that "although the 'native' Portuguese are loyal to the faith, nevertheless when heresy is so prejudicial and easy to communicate it is difficult to avoid" [96a].

The hatred borne by the New Christians is a "Jewish" hatred, according to the Report, which continues to make no distinction between Jews and New Christians. Their hatred toward Church and faithful impels these people to destroy the objects of their animosity at all costs, even at the risk of death, the Report says with the Church father, Jerome. When they cannot inflict physical harm, they follow the precepts of the Talmud to curse Christians.

The roots of this inveterate hatred are envy and innate greed, the Doctors say. But whatever the causes, it made the Jews the first persecutors of the Church, "crueler than the Neros and Diocletians." Far from abating, their hatred "has continued to this very day and will continue to the very end of the world," says the Report [97a–b]. It was prefigured in the biblical struggle between Isaac, representing the Christians, and Ishmael, representing the Jews (!).

This hatred causes the New Christians to inflict manifold material and spiritual damages on "good" Christians, and even "like thirsty harpies . . . they try to drink our blood" [98a]. New Christian physicians and pharmacists poison medicines or deliberately dispense wrong medicines, as a result of which popes and other authorities have frequently barred Jews from serving in such professions. In Portugal, "the instances of damage and death contrived upon their sick patients and confessed by them when penanced by the Inquisition are so many that it can never cease being a source of amazement that people still entrust them with their health" [98b].

Jews also kidnap Christian adults and children and visit every cruelty upon them, the Doctors relate. During Holy Week they even crucify a Christian with exquisite suffering. Their thirst for Christian blood is so great that when they lack available Christians to murder, they buy Christian captives in order to murder them. At the time of (the) Bar Kokhba (Rebellion 132–35 C.E.) they ritually murdered ninety thousand [sic] captives.[27] (John) Chrysostom calls them

---

27 This statement represents an embellishment of the document's stated source, Cesar Baronius. The passage in question may be found in Caesar Baronius, *Annales Ecclesiastici*, Augustino Theiner, ed.

"enemies of the human race," because in addition to taking all these lives, "they committed unbelievable horrors and atrocities. According to Eusebius, they ate their victims' flesh and daubed their faces with their blood. When they lack opportunities to murder Christians, they disinter their bodies from caves, something which even pagans regard as a sacrilege." According to one Christian author, they like "to offer the life and blood of Christians to the Devil. Others report that they mix the blood with herbs and fruits and drink it, anoint themselves with it on their deathbeds and keep it for other purposes" [99b–100a].

Their hatred has also impelled them to poison wells and fountains in their native lands and elsewhere. In addition, they have been involved in rebellions and mutinies as far back as the time of Constantine the Great. In Portugal, "where they should have shown themselves more benevolent and grateful because it had offered refuge to their harried ancestors expelled from other kingdoms, they committed their customary treasons and evils," the Doctors say. "It cannot be doubted," they continue, "that they are responsible for undermining all our conquests and bringing the Dutch, who are heretics and enemies of this Crown, to the Indies, and giving them the means to go to Brazil and capture the towns of Bahia and Pernambuco. Besides they help these same enemies with money to batter the ports and coasts of 'all Spain.'[28] Clearly indicative of all this is the corsairs' restitution of the properties they had robbed from the merchants among the New Christians, thus revealing that they are their confederates."

"Thus," the Doctors declare, "the New Christians are rebels, traitors and disturbers of the peace in all the kingdoms and republics in which they live.[29] In their bowels they harbor a mortal hatred even for those whom they externally treat with affection" [99a–b].

Further, say the Doctors, the Jews inflict great damage on Christian property. This, they claim, is the cause of Portugal's poverty and misery. This is to be contrasted with the New Christians' wealth, the result of their natural greed and avarice, recognized "in sacred and profane writings" [100b]. Wealth has always been the idol of the Jewish stock, the Doctors propose, even as far back as Israel's sins with the two sets of golden calves, the first in the Wilderness of Sinai, the second under Jeroboam.

Some nations expelled their burdensome Jews. France got rid of their usuries in the process. In Spain, the general expulsion of 1492 followed the destruction of various Jewish communities in 1328 and 1341 [sic] [101b].

(37 vols.; Paris: Barri-Ducis, L. Guérin, 1864–83) 2:214. The Report itself reads "Cosroas," but the section in Baronius dealing with Chosroes (10:296) does not discuss any alleged Jewish atrocities against Christians.

28 The term Espanha (España) referred to the entire Peninsula. See also, for example, below, pp. 67 and 68.

29 The text refers to riots in Navarre, Catalonia and various parts of Castile, all, of course, in Espanha.

Returning to Portugal, the Doctors declare, "One can judge how great the damages suffered by Portugal in this matter must be because through the hands of this people . . . travel all the merchandise and nearly all the contracts and leases which are made in Portugal. Thus in many ways the wealth of all of Portugal that should have been distributed among its natives ends up in their hands" [101b].

The New Christians also damage the honor of the native Portuguese. They depreciate Christianity as an impious heresy and maliciously impute crimes and falsehoods to Christians. Their embassies and letters are all directed to persuade others of this great blasphemy.

Their intention has been to shake the foundation of the Church, "against which neither the sword of tyrant nor the gates of hell can prevail" [102b], the Doctors affirm anomalously in the light of their own allegations of the spread of Judaism in the Peninsula, even among Old Christians. Despite all the inflammatory lies of the New Christians, the Doctors continue, Christianity has grown and spread and the Jews have been punished with suffering. Their murder of Christ led to their loss of all nobility and their notoriety as the worst people in the world, lower than the Egyptians and Assyrians. Emperor Tiberius (14–37 C.E.) said that little would be lost if they all died.

Their dishonor and infamy affected Portugal from the moment of their entry into the country, say the Doctors, equating Portugal's original Jews with its subsequent New Christians. That other nations regard the New Christians as Portuguese has therefore embarrassed the "true" Portuguese Christians. "We lose all the praise which our ancestors and many others merited," the Doctors dolefully conclude, "because in our midst we keep and honor the greatest enemies of the faith of Christ" [103a].

Even more serious, the Doctors believe, are the damages inflicted by the New Christians on the spiritual life of the Portuguese people, because these involve the salvation of their souls. To impede good Christians from this salvation, the "Jews" try everything within their power to swerve them from the true doctrine. They pervert Scripture by concealing its patent message of the coming of the Messiah. They obstruct the administration of the Holy Sacraments, this through ministers who are themselves heretical apostates (i.e., New Christians) and who therefore subvert baptisms, communions, and even marriages, where they frequently grant dispensations not authorized or specifically forbidden by the Church. They undermine churches by uttering blasphemies against saints, the cross, and even the images of Christ and the Virgin, as they have been doing from time immemorial.

They beat the image of Christ with the same hatred that their ancestors harbored toward the Savior. They buy consecrated hosts, toss them into fire, boiling water or cesspools, or stomp them or crush them with hammer and anvil, or, even worse, pierce them with daggers. All of these acts show their abhorrence of Christian sancta. Their cruelty was frequently betrayed by divine miracles: hosts bleeding from their perforations leaped from the fire or the cauldrons, blood rained from the heavens, and the earth quaked. Yet none of the Jews were thereby moved to confess their faults or seek pardon.

The money they lavish honoring the saints of the church also has an ulterior motive. "Experience has shown," the Doctors affirm, "that their intention is really to offer honors and celebrations to Queen Esther and the Patriarchs and the people who were burned for Judaism [by the Inquisition], whom they call martyrs, and to celebrate, honor and venerate those whom they cannot in public" [104b].

From this, the Doctors conclude, the descendants of these "Jews" may be expected to commit similar sacrileges with equivalent hatred and malice, and, they claim, this in fact has already occurred in various cities of Portugal.

No less damage is caused by the "Jews'" eagerness to proselytize. Already in biblical times, they scoured land and sea in this endeavor. In Portugal they proselytize by marrying Old Christians. As a result, "their children and descendants, because of the part of this venomous [Jewish] blood which touches them, are not only lowered in their nobility and lose it, but they are so inclined to follow the false superstitions [of their ancestors] to which any hint by a parent or any other relative is sufficient to persuade them. A single word in secret from a Jewish father is more effective for young girls than many years of their mother's upbringing in the doctrine of the Church" [105a].

At this point the Doctors make one of the most significant statements in their entire report: "But what compels greater fright and concern is that one-eighth or less and even a single drop of this blood has such power and force that it corrupts the entire body, no matter how honorable it might be. As a result, it frequently happens that at the first words of some old idiot, a nobleman, perhaps very learned, with very little Jewish blood, allows himself to be carried off [to Judaism]. After keeping the Law of Christ for many years, he turns to Judaism without reasons or arguments to persuade and convince him" [105a]. Indeed, the Doctors claim, eighty percent of all people who die at the stake have "a fourth or less" of Jewish blood [105b].

In addition, the Doctors observe, the greatest heretics and cruelest enemies of the Christian faith come from Judaism. Among them they mention Mohammed [sic]. According to some Christian authorities, he was of Jewish extraction and was instructed in Judaism by an uncle. He was so taken by the Jews that he used them to help compose the Koran, which therefore is greatly influenced by Jewish doctrine.

So also the "heretics from the North," meaning the Protestants, all have some connection with Judaism, the Doctors affirm. Even in times past a number of Christian heresies were so close to Judaism that the heretics frequently wanted to ally with the Jews or even become Jews.

Luther is said to have practiced Judaism before he persecuted the Church.

One Christian writer called Calvin "father of the Jews." Carolastadius[30] is included as a Jew because he wanted the Sabbath to be observed only on Saturday. So, too, is Martin Bucer. Being such great heretics, the Doctors suggest, they thought it worthwhile to participate in Jewish perfidy "so that they could become confirmed in wickedness" [106a].

Once again the Doctors return to the theme of "Jewish" hatred in order to emphasize its contemporary danger. Present in Portugal from the moment of the entry of the Spanish Jews and increased with their forced baptism and other events such as the time when they were put to the sword in the city of Lisbon [1506],[31] hatred by Jews is now further fueled by the New Christians' exclusion from important positions. But behind all this hatred lies the fact that "they are enemies of Christianity and the Christian people," and that "they have worked to destroy the republics and kingdoms in which they were born and live" [107a].

Another damage inflicted by the New Christians is the result of a beneficent government, the Doctors say. This gives New Christians opportunities to rise on the strength of their talents. It is interesting that they wish to stay on in Portugal even "with anxieties and fears in which they see themselves every day" rather than emigrate to places where they can live openly as Jews. The reason, the Doctors say, is simple. Portugal has good climate and food. It is also better suited to the business and mercantile interests of the New Christians than any other country because it is involved in maritime trade with all foreign nations. The New Christians derive so much advantage from this, according to the Doctors, that "they have taken all these business activities entirely into their own hands" [107b].

This explains the New Christians' monetary contributions for various communal purposes, the Doctors argue. Such contributions are intended to give the New Christians an acceptable public image and conceal their "blind and obstinate . . . love for Judaism."

Given these facts, their inveterate hatred for Christians and their desire to live openly and without anxiety as Jews, especially if they could continue to amass the monies they are now enjoying, "who can doubt," the Doctors rhetorically ask, "that it would be cheapest for them to buy their remedy by calling to their help some

30 The text reads "Carlos Tadio" a clear indication that the author or scribe did not realize that the Latin Carolastadius was a single name. It was used as a cognomen by the German Reformer, Andreas Bodenstein (ca.1480–1541) and derives from his birthplace, Carlstadt. See Frank Leslie Cross and Elizabeth A. Livingstone, eds., *The Oxford Dictionary of the Christian Church* (2d ed.; New York: Oxford Univ. Press, 1974) 240. See also John Nevins Andrews, *History of the Sabbath and First Day of the Week* (Battle Creek, Mich.: Steam Press of the Seventh Day Adventist Publication Society, [1862] 1873) 457.

31 In this connection see Yosef Hayim Yerushalmi, *The Lisbon Massacre of 1506 and the Royal Image in the Shebet Yehudah* (Cincinnati: Hebrew Union College Press, 1976).

of the enemies of the crown of Spain?" [108a]. Their constant communication and contacts with enemy nations are well known. New Christian agents in Portugal keep the enemy informed of everything that happens there. In view of Portugal's insufficiency of arms and ammunition, which are imported, and the defenselessness of its cities and villages, how could it withstand an enemy attack, especially if some of its forces were diverted to the defense of other places?

Taken together, these factors call for one immediate solution. That solution, the Doctors recapitulate, is nothing short of the expulsion of the New Christians from Portugal. They recall a letter written by the Archbishop of Valencia to Filipe II at the time of the expulsion the Moors from Spain,[32] explaining why this expulsion was just and necessary. The New Christians of Portugal present a far greater danger, the Doctors aver. They are much richer and much more numerous than the Moors were in Spain. The Moors could obtain aid only from other Moors and Turks, who could not easily attack Portugal, while New Christians can call heretics from the North to their confederacy. Besides, the Moors in all probability did not hate Christians as much, the Doctors propose. Yet the saintly Archbishop found it necessary to urge their expulsion. He even told the king that, if they were tolerated any longer, "all of Spain would be lost within his lifetime" [108b]. The Doctors remind us that at the time he wrote these words, the Archbishop was already sixty years old.

"What would this holy man say if he were informed of the great power held by the New Christians in Portugal, their wealth, their desires for vengeance, the extent of their Judaism and the means of their disposal to carry out treason?" the Doctors query. "Who would doubt that he would not more insistently urge that the kingdom be cleansed by a general expulsion or even that a harsher remedy be employed if necessary?" [108b]. It is obvious that the less drastic means which have been used so far have not been adequate, the Doctors argue.

The Recommendations of the Mythmakers

Standing in the way of the Doctors' solution were the six approaches variously favored by the New Christians. The Doctors themselves admitted that these had been "proposed by pious people [i.e., Old Christians] desirous of their [i.e., the New Christians'] salvation."

The Doctors categorically reject these proposals. "When the New Christians and the origins of their birth are considered," they say, the proposals turn out to be "more suited to ignite than extinguish Judaism." As a result, they continue, these proposals "have always been contemned by experienced and God-fearing people," by which they mean other Old Christians, "and impugned throughout

32 The reference is to the Moriscos, who were expelled from Spain from 1609 to 1614.

the kingdom, especially because the excess and daring of the people of the Nation never desist from inventing these and all other means they believe suitable for their intent"[109a].

The Doctors therefore find it necessary to provide a highly detailed refutation of each. In every case they lengthily repeat many of the arguments (and even the specific examples) they had already utilized in earlier sections of the Report. The substance of their arguments may be reduced to the following considerations:

1. The Doctors reject the need for an inspection of the Inquisition. The Inquisition is holy "in name and in works," they say. It has been responsible for the purity of the faith of the entire Iberian Peninsula. Its ministers are the most exemplary people in the entire kingdom and are in no way interested in the condemnation of the New Christians. On the contrary, they clearly perform the duty of serving as their counsel as well as that of compassionate judges in their blindness, because the New Christians are especially deserving of such concern. Besides, this is required by Christian charity and encouraged by Christian tradition. "How can the Inquisitors be called cruel?" the Doctors plead. "They relax only a few relapsed, impenitent heretics to the secular arm, and treat with full compassion all those who confess their sins and desire to become reconciled to the Church." But, the Doctors say, there is one sense in which the Inquisitors might justifiably be called cruel. "Although they know and admit that they regard most of the people reconciled to the Church as unregenerate offenders — it is quite evident to them because they see it in their confessions — they yet leave them among the rest of the faithful, and with this pestilence Christianity is obscured from that kingdom in the condition we perceive" [111b].

The New Christians' demand is frivolously conceived and maliciously grounded, the Doctors argue. Their intent is clearly not in the correction of an occasional flaw in the Inquisition's personnel or procedures. On the contrary, they aim to undermine the entire structure of the Inquisition. The mere accession to the New Christians' demands would be tantamount to an admission of at least the possibility of the alleged widespread corruption. Embellished by the New Christians' characteristic falsehoods and spread to the many countries where New Christians reside, any inspectional process would discredit the institution of the Inquisition throughout Christianity.

The New Christians also want to divert attention from their own misdeeds, in order "to cover the great scandal created in these times by the large number of heretics, apostates and *dogmatistas*[33] discovered among them and the numerous horrible sacrileges which are daily crying out to God and Your Majesty for punishment" [110b].

33 In the language of the Inquisition a *dogmatista* meant a teacher of heretical dogmas, especially those of Judaism, as it conceived Judaism.

So too the Doctors reject as specious the request for an inspection not only "by a person of high caliber and learning," but "if possible from outside the kingdom of Portugal, that he might be freer of all suspicion" rather than an indigenous inspector. The foreign inspectors requested by the New Christians would be unaware of the extent of their misdeeds and would be more corruptible than Portuguese inspectors, they insist. Besides, they wonder, how can evidence from "heretics and apostates . . . their relatives and supporters" [110a] be admissible?

The Inquisition has channels for processing complaints, but these channels have not been used, the Doctors insist. The introduction of the new mechanism of inspectorial visits would be regarded as a victory for the New Christians "at a time when the kingdom was aflame with Judaism" [110a], they conclude.

2. The Doctors reject the proposal for an automatic condemnation to death of everyone convicted of being a *dogmatista* in the broadest connotation of the word, that is, even including parents. They do so on the grounds of Christian charity, pointing out that it would be improper to apply the term to parents or relatives. "For a heretic to be called a *dogmatista*, they argue, "he must not only teach many people, but must do so with the title and in the capacity of a teacher." This is not so in the case of near kin, who are moved "by natural law" to teach their loved ones "what they believe, even if in error, to be necessary for their salvation" [111a–b]. Besides, the Pope would never become a party to the relaxation of first offenders who sincerely beg for reconciliation with the Church. The granting of such a request would prove counterproductive. To begin with, no one arrested by the Inquisition would acknowledge his indoctrination into Judaism by parents or relatives and thereby condemn them to certain death. As a result, many New Christians would die as *diminutos*. Furthermore, to save their parents, defendants would falsely implicate others. The Inquisition would furthermore be compelled to accept the testimony of single witnesses, namely the children secretly indoctrinated by their parents. This would be contrary to the New Christians' plea against the acceptance of testimony from singular witnesses.

All of this, the Doctors claim, suggests an ulterior motive on the part of the New Christians. Their intent can be nothing else than "to hide [all] the authors and teachers of their errors and greatly complicate the process of confession" [112b]. The net result, say the Doctors, would be to drive Judaism further underground, where it would thrive and grow.

3. The Doctors reject the proposal for a perpetual edict of grace. They note that the Inquisition already has the practice of admitting voluntary confessions and permitting reconciliation at all times "if the confessions are deemed to be true and with the zeal for salvation and if petition is made in writing to His Majesty

for a return of the confessor's possessions, which he grants with clemency and his accustomed favor" [112a–b]. To make such a policy independent of the king, they argue, would court religious delinquency. The reason that the New Christians have difficulty in this area is simply that their confessions are not really sincere, "since we observe that they do not change or improve in any way, as experience has shown." "Excessive clemency and favor," they say with St. Bernard, "is the mother of every insolence, the root of all incivility, and a license for laws to be broken with impunity." From various texts they reaffirm that "whoever makes no amends and does not want to leave his old customs of transgressing, deserves no pardon." Even more, that "whoever abuses privileges loses privileges" [113a].

4. The Doctors reject the proposal that would allow New Christians so inclined to sell their possessions, especially their real property, and leave the country. The supporters of this proposal hold that if New Christians of unimpeachable Catholic devotion wish to leave the country, there is no reason to deny them egress to whatever their destination might be. "And if on absenting themselves, they live estranged from the faith," they say, "it is better for them to leave and in this way not pervert others" [114a]. The New Christians' inability to leave Portugal at will, they complain, has made them fair game for false denunciations aimed at confiscating their possessions. Above all, they argue, the unfettered emigration of the New Christians would self-selectively rid the country of a large number of undesirables.

The Doctors, however, uphold the restrictive legislation. They regard it to be proper, harmless, and beneficial to the common good. They believe that it serves to strengthen faith and save souls. The Doctors impute this proposal to New Christian miscreants already accused or expecting to be accused before the Inquisition. Often, they say, it happens that "with the arrest of their relatives and friends who could expose them, they have sold their possessions, taken the money and gone over to the synagogues [i.e., the Jewish communities] of Salonika and Safed and the Rebellious States[34] and other places where they emerge openly as Jews and "infidels." Some have returned to the Peninsula as New Christians "better versed in the Talmud than if they had remained, with the resulting prejudice to all" [114b]. They have reappeared "with their names changed, coming as teachers and rabbis to instruct the rest. Even if they remain faithful [to Christianity], they still possess a proclivity to the [Jewish] Law" [114b].

34 The phrase "Rebellious States" refers specifically to the seven northern provinces of the Netherlands. Under the leadership of Holland and Zealand, they formed the Union of Utrecht in 1579, and two years later, proclaimed themselves independent from the Spanish crown. Equally common are the expressions "The Rebels' States," and simply "The Rebels." See, for example, Count Don Antonio, *Discourso en raçon de lo que pueden en general y particular los Reyes y Potentados contra esta monarchia y sobre el aumento della*, Ms. Biblioteca Nacional, Madrid, no. 4013, fols. 267–310, esp. ff. 295 a–b.

In the case of some New Christians who are not definitely committed to the practice of Judaism upon their departure from the Peninsula, "it could occur that when they go to a foreign kingdom where there are synagogues, they might easily become perverted and *the inclination which they have* may lead them to Judaize. *This reason and suspicion do not pertain for Old Christians nor can anyone question the freedom they possess*" [115a] (emphasis added).

At the same time, the Doctors point out, if free emigration were permitted, not all the New Christians would leave, and the problems caused by their presence would remain. Besides, the Doctors are not ashamed to admit, the king wants the New Christians to pay materially for their crimes, and "in detriment to the Exchequer not to hide their money or take it elsewhere" [115a]. The Doctors defend the right of sovereigns to control the movement of their subjects. They may determine the place of their travels and fix the length of their stay abroad. Likewise they may delimit "the alienation and sale of one's possessions." They even have the right to revoke agreements made if the benefit of the faith is involved.

The Doctors characterize previous royal privileges to the New Christians as exceptional and unenduring. They state that if the restrictive laws are to be lifted at all, it should be for a limited term and with the prohibition of any emigrant's return. They further reject the false denunciations adduced by the New Christians as a reason to lift the restrictions against them. Instead they call upon the king to remedy such situations, if indeed they exist, by tightening the enforcement of his laws "so that his subjects should not suffer extortion" [115b].

5. The Doctors reject the proposal to admit New Christians to public offices and honors. Both religious and secular law, they claim, reserve such dignities for people "noble in blood," with noble qualities deriving from unsullied ancestry. "No one doubts," they argue, "that magistracies and other high offices should be given to trustworthy and faithful people. The public burden rests on their shoulders. They bear responsibility for the shelter of widows, orphans and the unfortunate, the punishment of the guilty and the governance of the Republic. Rather than works," say the Doctors, playing with a basal theological distinction, "what is needed for this task is complete 'faith-fulness' (*fidelidade*)" [117b].

By these canons the New Christians do not qualify. "Though there are exceptions to the rule," the Doctors admit, the New Christians in general do not possess noble qualities but rather their opposites "in abundance." They are "of lowly and abject condition." They lack "a good lifestyle and praiseworthy habits" [116b]. They are constantly lusting after others' possessions and especially after gold, "which they adore as a god." They want to use such offices to enrich themselves and sell justice "to the highest bidder" [117a]. Through other avenues, they are already usurping the riches and undermining the well-being of the kingdom in their commerce and trade.

Besides, they bear "traces of the infamy their ancestors contracted in the death they inflicted upon the Redeemer, and, joined to it, the further infamy resulting from their inconstancy and the suspicion against them in matters of faith" [117b–118a].

There is considerable precedent for the denial of such honors and responsibilities to a group. In other kingdoms as well as Portugal there are laws which exclude commoners and certain types of lowly workers from such preferments. Such denial is especially important in the case of the New Christians, who are "foreigners and refugees" [118a]. Ever since they came, they have been a plague to Portugal. "Many religious and learned Old Christians," the Doctors affirm, "observe and regard as certain that after they [i.e., the New Christians] entered Portugal, sins became apparent which were formerly unknown" [117a]. They hold that "native-born citizens love the Fatherland and more zealously pursue the public good than the foreign-born, who do not possess this affection or know what is best for the governance of the land since they were not raised in it" [118a].

Besides, it would be unjust, the Doctors argue, "to take the bread out of the mouths of our sons" and give it to newcomers, especially "since the natives [!] ... won the Republic by the sword ... from the Moors, at the cost of considerable blood — which these people did not do, nor have they participated in our conquests, because they are not fit for war" [118a].

Haughty and wealthy, the New Christians are always trying to enter the noblest families of Portugal, the Doctors claim. The privileges they seek would even encourage Old Christians to intermarry with them to the great damage of the Republic, "since their vile blood leaves a perpetual stain on families ... *Any inferior blood, however small its amount, tarnishes and defames the generations of the nobles*" [118b], the Doctors orotundly proclaim (emphasis added). The Doctors mention with approval Portugal's inheritance laws. In order to preserve the families of nobility, these laws, under penalty of loss of inheritance — though the Doctors do not so explicitly state — prohibit the nobles' "children and successors from marrying people descended from the Jews or otherwise tainted by lowly blood" [118b–119a].

It is important for the Republic, the Doctors state, "that the nobles know who they are and that they be distinguished from humble people by recognizing the blood cleanness which they have inherited from their forebears. This cleanness becomes blurred and lost when the blood is mixed with that of lowly and infected people" [118a].

The New Christians' arrogance, the Doctors opine, should suffice to disqualify them from serving as judges. In such capacity they would vengefully display their hatred of Old Christians. Here especially one must consider their religious inconstancy and perfidy. Since their Judaism "is so rooted in their hearts, many of them in high places would be arrested by the Holy Office, and this would be a scandal for the Republic and a discredit to the offices of justice" [119a].

But the Doctors return to their principal argument. "If admitted to honors now," they say, "*it is unlikely that they will alter the inclination which is natural to them*" (emphasis added). On the contrary, they continue, if the New Christians' request is granted, there is reason to fear "that in a few years Judaism will have spread to the point where the entire kingdom and all Christianity will be ruined," and "the entire body of the nobility will be undermined and come to an end" [119b–120a].

Earlier churchmen in various councils approved marriages between converts from Judaism and other Christians "in order for Judaism to be extinguished," the Doctors concede. Yet, they insist, had they foreseen the extent of the New Christians' blindness and obstinacy and the dangers of their unregenerate inconstancy in matters of faith, they would have proscribed marriages between Old and New Christians. "Therefore," the Doctors offer, "we must appropriately state that they [i.e., the New Christians] bear the blame for the fact that there is no union between New Christians and Old and that they are despised. For divine, natural and civil law permit and obligate us to preserve our honor, the blood cleanness of our ancestors and the purity of our faith" [119b].

Attesting to the incandescence of the debate on the occupational discrimination against New Christians is the Report's extraordinary insert in this series of rebuttals of a special section at this point entitled "Answer to Opponents." At great length and with considerable logic of progression, the Report reorganizes, sharpens and focuses its arguments in a powerful offensive against the New Christians. If they have problems, they insist, it is their own fault. Apparently oblivious to their own repeated insistence on the unbridgeable hematological chasm between New Christians and Old, the Doctors briefly and contradictorily argue that there need not have been any distinction between them. Had the New Christians been faithful and constant, they say, had they accepted the kind and concerned efforts by previous Portuguese monarchs to confirm them in the Christian faith, there would have been no distinction between New and Old Christians. But experience has shown that the New Christians' blindness and obstinacy cannot be overcome. On the contrary "they continued in their superstitions." The Doctors' proposition here is that "since they [i.e., the New Christians] separate themselves . . . and the infamy of their apostasies is alive and growing daily with the perfidy of so many Judaizers, it would be a patent error to unite with people among whom those who appear just and good outwardly are the very ones who are haled into the Holy Office and whom we see emerging as penitents" [119b].

In rich detail, and with the weighty reinforcement of theological and practical considerations, the Report proceeds to review all its arguments against the admission of New Christians to public offices and honors. The thrust of these arguments is as follows: The Report implicitly takes the Paulinian denial of a distinction between Jew and Greek to mean that all people are equal. But it interprets this equality as belonging to the spiritual realm, to matters of conscience and the salvation of souls, and not to the temporal realm. Here, it points out, there are necessarily differences "in the estate of people," as one finds in the history of the Roman Empire and all other polities. "In society," it says, "there are freemen and slaves and there *are people of many castes* with whom it would be a dishonor for the citizen and men of quality to mix" [120a] (emphasis added). The inference could not be clearer: the New Christians are to be regarded as a caste.

The Report does not accept the historical documents that record the granting of honors to Jews by the Roman emperors. Commenting on a statement by Ulpian to this effect, it claims that the word "Jews" in the document really refers to Christians whom the pagan Romans called Jews! The Theodosian Code, the Report points out, clearly prohibits such benefits to Jews. That the New Christians are not like all other Christians with respect to their faith is evidenced in the declarations of various popes: Paul III (1534–49), Paul IV (1555–59), Sixtus V (1585–90), Gregory XIII (1572–85), Clement VIII (1592–1605), and Paul V (1605–21).[35] Realizing "the little confidence that could be had in the faith of the Hebrew people of Portugal, because of the frequent apostasies into which they fell," the Doctors aver, these popes disqualified them all from orders and ecclesiastical benefices. So did previous Portuguese monarchs, disillusioned that "they did not proceed with the necessary purity in matters of faith" [120b]. The history of the New Christians in Portugal shows them to be frequent and pertinacious recidivists in matters of faith. This was the case not only with the first converts; "The same holds true for their children and descendants, for we see that they retrogress. They abandon the [Christian] faith and are exactly like their ancestors in their customs" [122a].

Implicitly conceding that New Christians may have been given privileges, the Doctors recall that "this people is not disqualified because of the fact that they are [Christians] suspect in their [Christian] faith." This suspicion, they insist, extends to the group as a whole, to children, grandchildren and their descendants. It extends to all New Christians, including those among the secular and lay clergy and lay nobility. In apparent contradiction to their blanket condemnation of the New Christians as Judaizers, they recognize the possibility of a "rare, individual exception." Yet, they insist, "although in some cases the suspicion may end, and the people involved have merit, consideration should not be given to a deserving individual with the result that we break the law" [121a].

The Report goes to considerable lengths to demonstrate the incorrectness of the pro-New Christian contention that the exclusionary statutes are invalid, unjust and invidious. En passant it mentions that the statutes apply to descendants

35 This incorrect order is to be found on 120b. It may be corrected if we assume that the scribe inadvertently omitted Gregory XIV (1590–91) and incorrectly put the name of Gregory XIII in its place instead of where it belonged. One thing is clear: there was no confusion due to Roman numerals. All the Popes' numbers are given in Arabic numerals.

of both Moors and Jews, but it conveniently omits the telling fact that because of the New Christians' more sensitive sociopolitical location, it was they and not the *moriscos*, who were regularly targeted for exclusion.

The Doctors defend the validity of the statutes with an argument from tradition: Portugal has had a long skein of royal decrees prohibiting the advancement of New Christians to high office, they say. Furthermore, similar prohibitions have been adopted by various religious communities, schools and societies.

They defend the justice of the statutes with an argument from authority: In addition to their intrinsic justice, the Doctors aver, these statutes are acknowledged as just by leading churchmen, among them Gregorio de Simancas, Diego Velázquez and Ignacio de Villares.

The fairness of the statutes they defend with an argument from intention. The intention of the creators of these statutes leaves no doubt as to the loftiness of their purpose. "This intention becomes evident," they say, "if one considers that it is important to the state of the Republic and the conservation of the Faith of the Christian religion." Considering this purpose, there can be no doubt that in the issuance of these decrees, "all that was sought was to insure the tranquility of the people; the administration of justice, which is not safe in the hands of the aforementioned Hebrews; the separation of good people from contact with the bad; the preservation of the cleanness and nobility of our forebears and the avoidance of the trust of the sacred things and the ministry of the Church to people suspect in faith and of depraved habits" [123b].

6. The Doctors reject the proposal calling for a limited expulsion of the New Christians, to include those who have been reconciled to the Church and those abjured *de vehementi*. The Doctors admit that this proposal "could be supported with powerful arguments" [123b]. These arguments are aimed to demonstrate that with such an expulsion the ills of the kingdom would cease. The problem, claim the supporters of this proposal, stems from the incorrigible apostasy of the New Christians reconciled and, by implication, those abjured *de vehementi*. "Since ordinarily their conversion is feigned," they say, "they then with greater audacity communicate their errors to people of the Nation who listen to them." At the same time they continue their Judaizing, and if rearrested and condemned to the stake, they never reveal the identity of other Judaizers. The spokesmen for this proposal also claim that since it would serve the Church no less than the state, it could easily obtain papal approval. It would have the further advantage of obstructing facile communication between heretics. The biblical model for this, they suggest, is to be found in Abraham's expulsion of Hagar (Gen 21:10 ff.). Hagar, they say, represents the synagogue. "Therefore Sarah, illumined by the Holy Spirit, urged that the slave and her son be exiled . . . And because the expulsion of his son Ishmael appeared harsh to Abraham, God ordered him to listen to the voice of his wife" [124a].

The expulsion also has precedents in civil law, its proponents assert. To this effect they cite Cicero's statement, hardly unknown among the New Christians of Portugal, that "it is better for a limb to be lost than the entire body" [124a].[36]

In rebuttal, the Doctors characterize this proposal as defective "because it fails to indicate whether the expulsion is to be limited to those penanced or suspect *de vehementi* who leave the Holy Office or whether it will also include their children and grandchildren." The alleged purpose of this proposal, the Doctors state, is "to relieve and preserve the kingdom." Limiting the expulsion to New Christians who have confessed their crimes and those suspect *de vehementi* will not accomplish this purpose as long as their descendants, who are presumed to have been indoctrinated by them, remain in the country. "We would be left in the same condition and with the plague raging at home just as it had been" [124b]. The Doctors declare their opposition to this proposal even if it were broadened to include the children and grandchildren of the reconciled and *de vehementi* suspects. Such inclusion, they argue, would be unavailing. Knowing that they were doomed to exile, no members of the families of such people would volunteer any information about themselves or others because such cooperation with the Inquisition would not improve their lot. The Doctors conclude that none of the alternatives would be acceptable. They dismiss them all as "disposed to the conservation and concealment of Judaism rather than the provision of a remedy for it." They therefore proceed to commend their own solution, that all New Christians be expelled from Portugal. Only in this way, they claim, will it be possible to address "the supreme danger that may rightly be feared" and "the damage which the kingdom is suffering" [124b].

Yet, at every turn of the Doctors' discussion, it is evident that, their repetitive rhetoric notwithstanding, the Doctors did not actually envisage an expulsion of all the New Christians, or even necessarily all those convicted of Judaizing. This is seen in their concern with the continual denial of honors and offices to the New Christians; their acquiescence in the limitation of the expulsion to "the full people of the Nation," that is, those who are defined as full New Christians — a definition which, however conceived, had to clash with the fundamental concept of tainted blood — and their expectation of the continued threat of exile for New Christians who might stray into active Judaizing [121a–124b].

Emphasizing that if the scourge of Judaism remains unbridled it will "soon be impossible to remedy," the Doctors urge prompt action and, again in rich detail amply seasoned with reminiscences from Scripture and Christian tradition, they consider the two loci of responsibility for "Judaism to be extinguished" [125a].

36 Samuel Usque, *Consolation for the Tribulations of Israel*, Martin A. Cohen, trans. (Philadelphia: Jewish Publication Society of America, 1965, 1977) 229: ". . . for when a person's limbs are being devoured by herpes, it is best to cut them off with the knife or the fire, so as to prevent the spread of the disease and save the rest of the body. At such a time the cruel surgeon is the instrument of recovery."

The first is the religious locus, embodied in the Portuguese bishops. As bishops, the Report reminds them, their first obligation is that of "investigating the sins of their subjects and acquainting themselves with the most contagious vices," and then, "having identified them . . . to procure their remedy" [125a]. More than biblical priests enjoined to diagnose leprosy, the bishops, as Scripturally appointed sentinels, have the much more difficult task of diagnosing the diseases of the soul, visible as well as covert. Of these, the most serious, surreptitious, and contagious is heresy. "It is the one which most perturbs and destroys the Church" [126a] they say, and therefore it is the one that demands the greatest attention. Although the investigation of "the crime of heresy and the error of Judaism and other infidelities" has been delegated to the Inquisition, it is "because the bishops are otherwise occupied with various matters or because some of them are absent," but it remains the bishops' chief obligation. The Inquisition's role is in addition to that of the bishops. The bishops have in no way been absolved of their ordinary power in canon law. "This explains," the Doctors say, "why the prelates of this kingdom petitioned Your Majesty to deign to permit the convocation of a national council [of churchmen] or, at least, this Assembly, to be the better informed, with the help of scholars, of the errors of Judaism and to deal with their remedy."

In order to arrest sin and find means for the spiritual improvement of their subjects, the bishops' chief task is to conduct the necessary investigations leading to the exposure of all heresy. They must do so out of charity "not the kind that the individual should have toward his neighbor, but rather a charity more sublime and essential" [127a]. Their paradigm is Jesus himself, who regarded a detailed understanding of the sheep to be the chief duty of every shepherd.

Out of charitable concern for their flocks, the bishops must strive to uproot all heresy. If they do not stop it or even delay its extirpation, they are, as it were, accessories before the fact. Such, for example, was actually the charge made in the Book of Revelation against the Bishop of Pergamum in connection with his attitude toward the Nicolations. While he did not approve their heresy, he permitted others to follow it. Likewise the Israelite high priest Eli was punished "because although he rebuked his sons for their sins, his rebuke was not enough: he should have thrown them out of his house." So too "the kings who did not worship Jeroboam's idols, though praiseworthy, were censured for their negligence in not dashing them to the ground and thereby not blocking the possibility for others to engage in idolatry" [127b].

Bishops cannot plead innocence for inaction, the Doctors emphasize. "One cannot accept the shepherd's excuse that he did not pay attention to the wolf who ate the sheep" [127a]. To allow wrong to continue is tantamount to cooperation, aid and abetment. As judges and shepherds the bishops are obligated to defend their subjects; as spiritual fathers, they are obligated to teach and fortify them with Christian doctrine to keep them from the errors of heresy." If they do not do this, "they have gravely sinned and are worthy of retribution. What then shall be the punishment given to one who shall consent to the vices, not daring to reprove them or punish them?" [127b], the Doctors rhetorically ask.

Finally, the Doctors point out, Portuguese prelates would be remiss in their sacred obligations if they further refrain from stopping the spread of Judaism or delay "the remedy." By this they mean nothing short of the extirpation of the New Christians. Portugal's "Jewish problem" could have easily been dealt with when it arose, the Doctors claim. "How happier and more fortunate the Kingdom of Portugal would have been," they argue, "if, having admitted this plague of the Hebrews, it would have expelled them forthwith," because since that time Judaism "has grown and spread to such an extent in the kingdom that we are now compelled to struggle and fight against a giant so bold and daring that he now ventures to show his face and contend with the faithful" [128a–b]. Therefore "it is important that there be no further delay if we wish good results" [128a]. The bishops should "imitate what God did to stop the Israelites' intemperance in the desert," the Doctors suggest, "because He punished them at the time of their greatest fervor" [128a].

The second locus is the throne, to which the Report pays far greater attention than it does to the episcopate. Receiving his authority from the Church like the biblical monarchs from the priests, the king has the preservation of the Law of God and the Catholic faith as his first obligation. He assumes this obligation from the moment of his receipt of the symbolic sword from the bishop. Even more important than the natural good of his subjects, a king must through his laws seek their spiritual salvation. Furthermore, all the other qualities and virtues of princes "are of little worth, if they lack the zeal to ordain that their subjects preserve the Catholic faith and keep the law of God." No better example of this can be found than the case of Emperor Jovinian,[37] who renounced his empire "because he refused to govern people given to errors and superstitions" [129a]. Various codes of law and Church councils like the Sixth Council of Toledo under King Chintila (636–39) have made princes swear to this defense as their paramount priority.

This obligation is particularly incumbent upon the Portuguese monarchs, the Report continues, "because God granted them the kingdom, taking it out of the hands of the Moors with miraculous victories, on condition that the

37 The reference has to be to Jovian, the short-lived Christian emperor who succeeded to the Roman imperial throne shortly after the death of Julian the Apostate on June 26, 363 and ruled briefly and unhappily until his death (not resignation) on February 16–17 of the following year. The background of the legend of his resignation may derived from the fact that Valens, named co-emperor by Jovian's successor, Valentinian, issued edicts of religious toleration in line with the policies of Emperor Julian. See, e.g., Guglielmo Ferrero and Corrado Barbagallo, *A Short History of Rome*, George Chrystal, trans. (2 vols.; New York: [Putnam, 1919]; Capricorn Books, 1945) 2:451–52.

faith be preserved in its full purity and Christian piety" [130a]. The faith was so preserved before Joao II's admission of the Jewish refugees from Spain. Until then Portugal had no enemies and God's promises for its glory were fulfilled, "because there were not among us the errors and heresies which were found in other kingdoms, or any teacher to teach them. Nor by the grace of God will there ever be at any time among *the native Portuguese*, for God had chosen them to carry His name to very remote parts of Asia, Africa and Brazil, where apostolic men have sown the faith with the fruitful result that we see innumerable souls observing the Law of Christ and acknowledging the Church, though they live so far away" [130a] (emphasis added).

The reason for Portugal's good fortune was that King Filipe (I = Felipe II of Spain), grandfather of the present king, repressed the Lutheran (i.e., Protestant) heresy with fire and sword when it made it first appearance in some of his territories. Therefore, since Judaism is so widespread, it is His Majesty's duty to order the speedy application of the remedies necessary for its termination and extinction" [130b].

Furthermore, going back to their investiture by biblical priests, kings were made to understand that they were to be guided by the priesthood. Even when Herod wished to learn whether Christ had been born, he sent not for his counselors of state but for the priests and doctors of the Law, "because he was persuaded that since the matter was spiritual and divine and related to the Law, it belonged to the priests and the doctors" [130b].

And the Doctors declare, "if such was the subordination and respect of the princes of the Old Law toward the priests of that time, should not Christian princes have the same respect for the prelates of the Law of Grace, on whom God more liberally showered knowledge and wisdom so that they should not err fundamentally in matters pertaining to the Christian religion?" [131a].

Especially in matters involving heresy, the king should seek counsel from "the most appropriate counselors," namely the bishops. The Report cites with approval John Chrysostom's opinion that a prince should not wait for the prelates of the church to seek him out. Rather "he should send for them and follow their advice" [131a–b].

The Portuguese monarchs have always been governed by the bishops in matters of conscience. Even more, they have left the election of their successors to their discretion.

Rulers are also known as avengers. They must punish evils committed against the Republic. The Doctors regard the Greek king, described by Strabo as harsh beyond all bounds, to have been virtuous in the administration of his office.[38]

---

38 This appears to be a paraphrastic reference to Cassander (ca. 354–297 B.C.E.), king over the Macedonians (301–297). See: Horace Leonard Jones, ed. and trans., *The Geography of Strabo*, LCL IX:1:20 (London: W. H. Heinemann–New York: G. P. Putnam) 4:268–69.

They applaud King David's statement in Psalms (101:8): "In the morning I shall slay all the sinners of the earth." David took the life of the sinners with his own hand, regarding this act as a whole offering to God. The Doctors also admire Hugh Cardenal's observation that, when Moses crossed the Red Sea, he "drowned all the wicked in the first part of the day, because it was fitting that he who was to give them [i.e., his people] light so that they might fully dedicate themselves to God, should first remove all the impediments with the sword of justice" [132a–b].

Moses also told the Levites: "You have consecrated your hands unto the Lord" when he saw their hands dyed red with the blood of their sacrifices. The prophet Samuel killed Agag with his own hand, while King Ferdinand the Saint[39] "did not disdain . . . to carry in his own hands the firewood to burn the heretics of his own kingdom" [132b].

When Christian princes occupied themselves zealously with the defense of the faith, the Report goes on to say, "they had happy results and God prospered them in their estates and conquests" [132b], using other rulers as instruments of His will in their behalf. But, at times, princes fail in this obligation because of "indiscreet pity and compassion" [133b] for their subjects. King Saul's misfortune stemmed from his sparing of Agag the Amalekite (1 Samuel 15). And more than for any other reason, King Ahab lost his kingdom because of the pity he showed for (Ben-hadad), the king of Syria (1 Kings 20). Unwarranted clemency, the Report cautions, is not the will of God. "God not only inculpates us for granting mercy and pardon to those whom He orders to be punished; He does not even want us to mourn for them or have any pity for them" [134a]. Not only that, but if princes fail to defend God's will and God's Church in this obligation, "God will render account from them, because the faith gains through the solicitude of the good just as it loses through the negligence of the wicked" [133b]. "When you see a kingdom declining in prosperity and commerce, in vigor and courage, and it seems that heaven shows itself in everything unfavorable — the earth denies it its fruits, the sea its lanes —" the Doctors declare following Ambrose, "these losses and misfortunes are not be attributed to sea, earth and sky." "The cause of the misfortunes," they suggest, lies in "the secret abominations, sacrileges, excesses and the failure to punish them" [133a].

The Doctors cite St. Bernard's complaint to Pope Innocent III that he was lax in the punishment of the wicked. Bernard reminds Innocent that "God ordered all the apostles and preachers to fish with nets which, without killing the fishes, bring them to the land. But St. Peter, whose successor he [Innocent] was, was ordered to fish with a hook, which wounds and kills . . ."[40] [134a].

39 B. 1201 (?), d. 1252. King of Castile (1217–52) and King of Leon (1230–1252). It was during his reign that the Christian forces broke the back of Moslem control in the Peninsula with the capture of most of Andalusia.

40 The reference is to Matt 17:27.

The Doctors proceed *a fortiori* to strike at the New Christians. "If, in the case of a Pontiff, whom God more appropriately armed with a staff than with a sword, He demands this through the coactive power which he possesses," they say, "what does He expect His Majesty to do with the people of the Nation in his kingdom who, though they are baptized Christians, so publicly profess Judaism, blaspheme His holy name, commit horrendous sacrileges against His most holy person, and, above all this, falsely and arrogantly boast of having more protectors than adversaries and of being better heard than those who expose their wickedness in the defense of the faith and seek the remedy therefor?" [134b].

God has ordained "a very different treatment" [134b] for this people, the Doctors assert. In accordance with the biblical curse, "They who condemn Me will be base" (1 Sam 2:30), they are to be outlawed, suppressed, perpetually enslaved by the nations, and condemned to wandering in fear like Cain until their ultimate destruction. These curses, the Doctors insist, are not limited to "the Jews who had not yet received the Faith," but to the "faithless enemies . . . Christians in name . . . the Jews of this kingdom" [134b].

Another reason why princes fail in this obligation to destroy evildoers is their own desire for material gain. This prompted Saul to his act of disobedience to God's will that he kill Agag the Amalekite. Equivalent acts by contemporary princes cause greater evils in a republic because they create "the opportunity for punishment to be flouted and criminals to increase" [135a]. The problem is severe in Portugal. "Nor is it our intention to say that the [king's] ministers [as a group] have an interest in concealing the evils of Judaism and conceding benefits and favors to some people of the Nation," the Doctors state. "But, it is possible that someone [among them] is advising His Majesty to keep this people in his realms because they are very rich and powerful merchants and they provide monies for public needs and because it may be feared that if we expel them, the advantage will accrue to the enemies of the Church and of these realms of *Espanha* with whom they would ally" [135a]. Once again they liken the situation to Saul's disobedience to God in the sparing of Agag as a result of the counsel of many soldiers in his army, "carried away by greed and desire of personal gain, who persuaded the king not to kill Agag and not to burn the spoils as God had commanded him" [135a].

The implications for Portugal are clear, the Doctors suggest. The fear of losing temporal things should be swept aside, and God's will followed. On this note they return to the laudation of the piety of King Filipe III (Felipe IV of Spain), which they regard to have been demonstrated in his rejection of the recent New Christian offer of considerable sums of money for his consideration of their request for another general pardon. Praising him for the fact that "together with [noble] blood and the greatness of estate, he inherited from his royal predecessors the scorn of personal gain, sacrileges and offerings of money" [135b], the Doctors recall the rejection by the Visigothic King Reccared (586–601) of monies offered him by the Jews if he would abrogate a discriminatory law he had promulgated against them and the consequent praise this elicited from St. Gregory. It also reminded St. Gregory of King David's rejection of a glass of water offered him during his thirst [2 Samuel 23:16]. King David poured it out, or rather, consecrated it "as a libation to God" [135b–36a]. The Saint concluded that "if a small goblet of water which David refused to drink and offered to God had such value for him that he regarded it as a sacrifice, how much more would God esteem the rejection of money which the King refused to accept only out of respect for Him?" [136a].

The connection of the entire argument to King Filipe and God's relationship to his kingdom is then clearly drawn: "since His Majesty despises the gold and monies which the people of the Nation offer him to attain pardon for the errors they have committed without any intention of mending their ways, and to attain offices and dignities from which they are excluded since they are unworthy of them, this great sacrifice will be acceptable to God. And in reward thereof, in spite of the envious, may the monarchy of Espanha increase and prosper with miraculous success" [136a].

The Doctors then offer a pointed summary of the position. "Let us again establish and regard as certain," they begin, "that His Majesty not only can but is obligated in conscience to carry out the civil, vindicating and remedial punishment of the community and people of the Nation of this kingdom by exiling and expelling them, with confiscation of property, at least in the case of the 'full' persons of the Nation, because all the aforementioned reasons and considerations are evidenced in them, especially those concerning the corruption and contagion of Judaism which these full New Christians in particular teach, perverting the others. There is no probable hope for them to be reclaimed and converted as there can be in the case of those who are not full New Christians, because of their admixture of good blood. These could indeed entertain such hope if they were not exposed to the leading teachers of Judaism, the authors of their belief, and if they would see that by not keeping perfectly the Law of God they are going to receive the same penalty of expulsion and exile from the kingdom . . ." [136a].

The Doctors conclude that "in this way it appears that support will be given to the goals that we should have, which are the conservation of this kingdom in the purity of the faith, the punishment of transgressions committed against it and the conversion of those who are considered susceptible of correction" [136a].

Analysis

From an examination of its contents, it is obvious that the Report of the Assembly of Tomar can by no stretch of the imagination be regarded as objective. From its doctrinaire introduction to its rhetorical conclusion, it leaves no doubt of its construction on passion and parti pris. Its tenacious defense of the Inquisition, its idealization of the Inquisition's manifold activities, its unmitigated hostility to all New Christians, its intemperate condemnations of their character and actions, and its categorical refusal to countenance even the slightest of their claims, complaints or suggestions, lead ineluctably to the conclusion that the scholars and bishops assembled at the Convent of Christ came there not with open minds, but with preconceived judgments, and, even if in embryo, a predetermined course of action.

Eloquently witnessing to the gravity of the "Jewish problem" as they perceived it was the expenditure of the not inconsiderable funds and man-hours involved in the lengthy three and a half month convocation. Attesting to it no less dramatically throughout the Report they submitted is the elaborate mythicization of the New Christians into the "Enemy" of the Portuguese people. This mythicization holds the key to the significance of the Assembly of Tomar.

In this mythicization, simplistic and reductive like all others of its kind, the New Christians, without exception, are depicted as irremediably evil, while all Old Christians are unalloyedly good. As frequently throughout history, the two polarities of Good and Evil are here once again locked in apocalyptic battle, with Evil attacking and gaining and Good thrown back to its final defense. Besides, while the good stand in constant danger of contamination by Evil's elan, evil is impervious to the penetration of Good. The sources of good and evil alike lie in the mystery of the blood with its "communication . . . and transmission from parents to children."[41] The blood of the good is pure and clean, the blood of the evil impure and unclean. Purity and cleanness of blood are the result of unsullied Christian ancestry. Impurity and uncleanness derive from the admixture of Jewish blood. However remote a Christian's Jewish forebear and however minuscule his "percentage of Jewish blood, even if limited to a single drop"[42] a Christian is tainted and possessed by its demonic power.

---

41 Report of the Assembly of Tomar, fol. 46b.

42 See Fray Agustín Salucio, *Discurso . . . acerca de la justicia y buen gobierno de España en los Estatutos de limpieza de sangre y si conviene o no alguna limitación en ellos* (ca. 1600): ". . . Para tener raça basta un rebisabuelo judío, aunque los otros 15 sean rechristianísimos. Pues en qué seso cabe creer que el rebisnieto a de sacar la lançada del infiel más que la bondad de los 15 calificados . . . ?" The quotation, taken from fol. 13r of the manuscript, is found in Eugenio Asensio, "El erasmismo y las corrientes espirituales afines," *Revista de filología española*, 36 (1952) 65.

The demonic element in unclean, or "Jewish" blood, is discharged in its perversion of Christians toward Jewish belief and practice, regardless of the strength of their Christian indoctrination or the devoutness of their Christian practice and profession. Every New Christian, even if not actively or consciously associated with Judaism, is therefore nevertheless a potential Judaizer. Every New Christian is a member of the "People of the [Hebrew] Nation," and as such, incapable of being a "native Portuguese." Every New Christian, whether or not perceptibly deviant in matters of faith, is radically a heretic, and a target for the vulgar term *Marrano*, or "pig."[43]

The first documentary manifestation of the *"Marrano Myth"* appeared a hundred and eighty years before the Assembly of Tomar. It came in the form of a pronouncement of questionable legality, issued on June 5, 1449, a few days after a carefully planned but ostensibly spontaneous outburst of violence against the New Christians in Toledo. This pronouncement is known as the *Sentencia-Estatuto*. The *Sentencia-Estatuto* stigmatized all New Ch ristians as Jews on the basis of descent. As such, it claimed, they were irresistibly drawn to the Jewish religion and hostile to all things Christian. The avowed intent of the document was to declare New Christians unfit for public office and honors.[44]

In the decades that followed, the *Sentencia-Estatuto* stimulated exclusionary provisions throughout Spain. These were applied to guilds, schools and colleges, religious and military orders and cathedral chapters. They even led to prohibitions of marriages between New and Old Christians. Culminating this process was the ratification by both Pope Paul IV in 1555 and King Felipe II of Spain in 1556 of the exclusionary statute adopted in 1547 by the Cathedral of Toledo at the initiative of its fiery archbishop, Juan Martínez Silíceo. Defenses of this statute written by Silíceo himself (1549), Diego de Simancas (1575) and Baltasar Porreño (1608) developed the implications of blood cleanness (*limpieza de sangre* in Spanish, *limpeza de sangue* in Portuguese) and fleshed out the Marrano myth.

43 On the word "marrano," see Martin A. Cohen, "Marrano," *EncJud* (16 vols.; New York–Jerusalem: Macmillian, 1971–72) 11:1018 and the bibliography therein contained. See also Yakov Malkiel, "Hispano-Arabic marrano and its Hispano-Latin homophone," *Journal of the American Oriental Society,* 68 (1948) 175–84 and Arturo Farinelli, *Marrano: Storia di un vituperio* (Geneva: L.S. Olschki, 1925). The etymology of the term is obscure; yet, whatever its derivation, its conjuration of a pig remains its most likely concretization. Derivations from the word "marrar," meaning "to spoil," such as the one where a New Christian explains that he is called a marrano, because he erred in changing from the good faith (Christianity) to the bad faith (Judaism) appear to be ad hoc and folk derivatives that require investigation and discussion beyond our present concerns. On this see Carlos Carrete Parrondo, *El tribunal de la Inquisición en el Obispado de Soria (1486–1502)* (*Fontes Iudaeorum Regni Castellae*, 11) (Salamanca: Univ. Pontificia de Salamanca, [Granada]: Univ. de Granada, 1985) 53.

44 For a full appraisal, including bibliography, of the *Sentencia-Estatuto*, see now Eloy Benito Ruano, *Los orígenes del problema converso* (Barcelona: Ediciones El Albir, 1976) esp. 39–83. The text of the *Sentencia-Estatuto* may be found on pages 85–92.

At the same time Spanish polemical works from Alfonso de Spina's *Fortalitium Fidel* (1461) to Francisco de Torrejoncillo's *Centinela contra judíos* (1673) and beyond, racistically applied the vast store of medieval anti-Jewish canards to their New Christian contemporaries.[45]

The Portuguese were well aware of the myth as it developed, and Portuguese polemics like João de Barros (16),[46] Francisco Machado (16),[47] João Baptista d'Este (17),[48] and Vicente da Costa Mattos (17),[49] made ample use of its implications.

Like all other myths, the "Marrano myth" in the Report of the Assembly of Tomar can be expected to contain a bedrock of reality beneath its gossamer of fabrication. Invariably such sub-mythical reality reflects crisis and struggle. The purpose of the gossamer is to soften, deflect and, to the extent possible, conceal this reality for the purposes of the myth's individual or corporate fabricators. Included in the reality to be concealed are the fabricators' real motives and frequently their identity.

This reality is always complex, as complex as human society always is, particularly when in crisis. It is never monodimensional, never exclusively ideological, economic or political, even though the myths may exaggerate one of these areas — usually the ideological — to the reduction or even exclusion of the others. It is rather always an indissoluble compound of all major dimensions

45 For a thorough discussion of these works see Albert Sicroff, *Les controverses des statuts de "pureté de sang" en Espagne du xv au xvii siècle* (Paris: Didier, 1960) 167–70. For a survey of limpieza de sangre see also Henry Kamen, *The Spanish Inquisition* (London: Weidenfeld and Nicolson, 1965) 122–39. Among the abundant documentation for this racist position see the *Perfidia Judaica ... Discurso Iurídico e Político* (n.d.: n.p., n.a.), ms. in António Joaquim Moreira's *Colecção de papeis impressos e manuscritos originaes mui interessantes para conhecimento da História da Inquisição em Portugal I* (Lisbon: Biblioteca Nacional, 1863) Cód. 867, fols. 190–226, esp. fol. 192a: "All people descended and infected from the Hebrew nation ... all have the same blood ... all profess the same customs" (trans. mine). The notoriety of this position is best evidenced by its record in popular literature. Of the innumerable available examples, see, v.g., the Portuguese *Letter to Licenciado Jorge Mendes Nobre, written by a Friend after he [the former] emerged from an auto-da-fé in penitent's garb, December 19, 1703*, ms. in *Colecção Pombalina* (Lisbon: Biblioteca Nacional, n.d.) vol. 68, fols. 95a–6a, esp. 18 c–d, "That a soul in the body of a Jew/cannot be a devotee of Christ" (trans. mine).

46 See Innocêncio Francisco da Silva, *Diccionário Bibliográphico Portugugêz* (23 vols.; Lisbon: Imprensa Nacional, 1858–1923) 3:318–23 and João de Barros's *Diálogo evangélico sobre artigos de fé contra o Talmud dos Judeus*, Israel Salvator Révah, ed. (2 vols.; Lisbon: Livraria Studium Editora, 1952–55) with Révah's comprehensive introduction, 2:xi–xc.

47 *Espelho de Christãos Novos*, written in 1541 and edited and translated from its unique manuscript (Biblioteca Nacional, Lisbon, *Colecção-Fundo Geral*, Ms. 6747) with the title *The Mirror of the New Christians* by Mildred Evelyn Vieira and Frank Ephraim Talmage (Toronto: Pontifical Institute of Medieval Studies, 1977).

48 On João Baptista d'Este, a convert from Judaism, see Silva, *Diccionário*, 3:303–4. See also *Papel que fez João Baptista de Este, de nação hebrea, que convem botar destes Reynos de Portugal os christãos novos. 21 Agosto 1619*, Arquivo Nacional da Torre do Tombo, Cód. 1506.

49 On Vicente da Costa Mattos, see Silva, *Diccionário*, 7:423–24.

of life and their intertwining nuances. The crisis it reveals inevitably involves struggles, and while these are not bereft of idealism, they all simultaneously entail a quest for position and power.

To unravel this gossamer and piece together the reality from the documentary sherds that have survived the ravages of time becomes the task of the historian. Only when the task has been completed can the historian proceed to the basal problem of reconstructing the motivation and identity of the mythmakers.[50]

The unraveling process typically begins by exploding a myth with its own contradictions. The explosion can be most easily accomplished by puncturing the myth at the point of its cardinal assumptions. In the case of the Report of the Assembly of Tomar, the telling punctures can be made on three of its basic propositions:

First, that all or nearly all Portuguese New Christians were Judaizing in the late 1620's. If so, why did the Inquisition fail to prosecute them? According to an Inquisitorial report of 1624,[51] there were 200,000 New Christian homes in

---

50 For a more detailed discussion of the philosophy and examples of such reconstruction see the author's studies: "The Role of the Shilonite Priesthood in the United Monarchy of Ancient Israel," *HUCA* 36 (1965) 59–98; "The Rebellions During the Reign of David," *Salo Wittmayer Baron Jubilee* (3 vols.; New York: Columbia Univ. Press, 1974 [1975]) 2:263–85; the revised version of the same article, *Journal of the Central Conference of American Rabbis,* 22:4 (Fall 1975) 13–34; "In All Fairness to Ahab: A Socio-Political Consideration of the Ahab-Elijah Controversy," *Eretz-Israel* 12 (1975) 87–94; "Anan ben David and Karaite Origins," *Jewish Quarterly Review (N.S.)* 68 (1977–78) 139–45, 224–34; "The Prophets as Revolutionaries," *Biblical Archaeology Review* 3 (1979) 12–19; *Two Sister Faiths: Introduction to a Typological Approach to Early Rabbinic Judaism and Early Christianity* (Worcester, Mass.: Assumption College, 1985) 1–7; and "Dimensions socio-politiques des origines et du developpement du Karaisme," in Shmuel Trigano, ed., *La Société juive a travers l'histoire* (4 vols.; Paris: Fayard, 1992) 1:399–425. For the applications of sociopolitically sensitive methodologies to the New Christians, see especially Ellis Rivkin, whose pioneering work in this area chronologically and conceptually must be accorded pride of place, especially his seminal essay, "The Utilization of Non-Jewish Sources for the Reconstruction of Jewish History," *Jewish Quarterly Review* 48 (1957) 183–203; his *The Shaping of Jewish History* (New York: Charles Scribner's Sons, 1971) 140–60; his essay "How Jewish Were the New Christians," *Hispania Judaica,* Joseph Silverman, Samuel G. Armistead and Josep María Sola Solé, eds. (2 vols.; Barcelona: Puvil, 1980) 2:105–15, and its bibliographical apparatus. Insight into the nuances of Rivkin's philosophy can be observed in the numerous reviews of scholarly works in the field, among them his review of Benzion Netanyahu's *Abravanel, Statesman and Philosopher* (Philadelphia: Jewish Publication Society of America, 1953) in *Judaism* 3 (1954) 267–70; Netanyahu's *The Marranos of Spain: From the Late 14th to the Early 16th Century* (New York: American Academy of Jewish Research, 1966) in *American Historical Review* 72 (1967) 7–9; Sicroff, *Les controverses* in *Commentary* (June, 1962) 544–47; and Yosef Hayim Yerushalmi's *From Spanish Court to Italian Ghetto* (New York: Columbia Univ. Press, 1971) in *Canadian Historical Review* 7 (September, 1972) 187–88.

51 See Arquivo Nacional, Inquisição, vol. 1605, fol. 211. This document is reproduced in Azevedo, *Cristãos Novos,* 471–72. See also Azevedo, *Elementos para a História Económica de Portugal (Séculos XII a XVII)* (Lisbon: Gabinete de Investigações Económicas do Instituto Superior de Ciências Económicas e Financeiras, 1967) 161. The claim of 200,000 families is by no means an exaggeration, as Azevedo states, but rather a reasonable estimate based on the large number of marriages between

Portugal. This indicates a New Christian population of around a million, or approximately half the total population of Portugal at that time. To be sure, the Portuguese Inquisition did increase its activity in the 1620's; but the half dozen major autos-da-fé during that period yielded fewer than a thousand convicts.[52] Since the Doctors of Tomar were not only devout Catholics but devotees of the Inquisition, it can hardly be assumed that they would have flouted the Inquisition's publicized demand that people with knowledge of heretics denounce them or face arrest themselves.

Furthermore, of all the convicts during these years, fewer than fifty received the supreme penalty. All the others were reconciled to the Church.[53] The

---

Old Christians and New Christians and the at least theoretical inclusion of all their descendants into the New Christian category.

52 The inquisitors themselves admitted that not all New Christians Judaized. See, for example, Adler, "Les Marranes d'Espagne et de Portugal," *Revue des Études Juives* 50 (1905) 217.

53 Azevedo, *Cristãos Novos*, 171–92. The position that the New Christians were in fact, with expected rare exceptions, striving to devote themselves to the faith of their own or their ancestors' conversion was advanced by leading Catholic voices from the time of the promulgation of the *Sentencia-Estatuto*. It is implicit as early as September 24, 1449 in the bull issued by Pope Nicholas V, declaring all the Christian faithful to be one and reaffirming the laws of Alfonso X of Castile (1252–84) and his successors which made converts eligible for the privileges available to all Christians. (See Henry Charles Lea, *A History of the Inquisition in Spain* (4 vols.; New York: The Macmillan Company, 1901; repr. New York: AMS Press, 1966) 1:127. Such support of the New Christians was advocated by leading prelates in both Spain and Portugal until the suspension of the Spanish and Portuguese Inquisitions.

For the major directions of previous reconstructions see Netanyahu, *The Marranos,* esp. 1–4; José António Saraiva, *Inquisição e Cristãos Novos* (5th ed.; Lisbon: Editorial Estampa, 1985) now in the process of publication in English translation under the title *The Marrano Factory: The Portuguese Inquisition and its New Christians,* with introduction, notes and appendixes by Herman Prins Salomon and Issac S. D. Sassoon; Martin A. Cohen, "Toward a New Comprehension of the Marranos," *Hispania Judaica* (1980) 1:23–5 and "The Sephardic Phenomenon: A Reappraisal," in Martin A. Cohen ed., *Sephardim in the Americas* (Cincinnati: American Jewish Archives, 1992) constituting a special issue of *American Jewish Archives* (vol. 44) and subsequently reprinted under the editorship of Martin A. Cohen and Abraham J. Peck (Tuscaloosa, Alabama: Univ. of Alabama Press, London, 1993) 30–54. The problem is well summarized by Anita Novinsky, *Cristãos Novos Na Bahía* (São Paolo: Editora Perspectiva, 1972) 3–15 and in her essays, among them notably, her "Sistema de poder e repressão religiosa: para uma interpretação do fenómeno Cristão Novo no Brasil," *Anais do Museu Paulista* 29 (1979) 5–12. In the latter study, for example, Novinsky correctly points to the differences between the Spanish and Portuguese Inquisitions (pp. 11–2). These differences must be analyzed alongside the basic elements held in common by the Inquisitions of Spain, Portugal and their dependencies as well as the factors which differentiated them from the medieval Inquisition and their contemporary Inquisitions in Italy. These considerations however, transcend the confines of our present investigation.

The position of the continued devotion to Judaism by most, or even all of the converts, is found in Fritz (Itzhak) Baer, *A History of the Jews in Christian Spain,* translated from the Hebrew by Louis Schoffman (2 vols.; Philadelphia: Jewish Publication Society of America, 1966) 2:246 (". . . the *conversos,* whose number ran into tens of thousands, and most of whom were Jews in fact") and

Inquisition's surveillance of reconciled heretics being particularly tight, it is more reasonable to assume that the good fortune of the vast majority in this regard was due to the sincerity of their reconciliation to the Church rather than the successful concealment of their recidivist Judaism, as the purveyors of the myth doctrinairely contended. Besides, why, contrary to the Report's explicit claim, did so few New Christians become Jews when they left Portugal? Exact figures are difficult to come by, but when one reconstructs from the realities of the Portuguese New Christian Diaspora rather than from the exaggerated claims of the opponents of the New Christians, it becomes evident that during the entire Inquisitorial period of two and three-quarter centuries, the total number of Portuguese New Christians who became Jews on leaving Portugal could not have exceeded fifteen thousand,[54] and may have been considerably less. This figure, of course, does not include their descendants born abroad. By any reckoning, this is only a fraction of the total number of Portuguese New Christian emigrés during this time. One of the cardinal works of Jewish theology of the sixteenth century, the *Consolation for the Tribulations of Israel* (1553), written by the former New Christian Samuel Usque, who had openly embraced Judaism in Italy, was directed to the New Christians in Italy "recently pursued and routed from the realms of Portugal," and "vacillating in their faith — most out of the too little constancy which has resided in our spirits from the very beginning."[55] The

---

in the manifold studies of Israel Salvator Révah, for example, "Les Marranes," *Revue des Études Juives* 1 (= 118) (1959–60) 29–77. See also two seminal studies by Gérard Nahon, "Les Sephardim, Les Marranes, Les Inquisitions Péninsulaires et leurs archives dans les travaux récents de I.–S. Révah," *Revue des Études Juives* 132 (1973) 5–48 and "Les Marranes espagnols et portugais et les communautés juives issues du marranisme dans l'historiographie récente," *Revue des Études Juives* 136 (1977) 297–367. This position continues to find support from distinguished scholars. See, for example, Joseph Kaplan, "The Portuguese Jews in Amsterdam: From Forced Conversion to a Return to Judaism," *Studia Rosenthaliano* 15 (1981) 37–51. The persistence of the traditional appraisal of the Marrano myth continues in works like Sonia A. Siqueira, *A Inquisição Portuguesa e a Sociedade Colonial* (in Brazil) (São Paolo: Editora Atica, 1978) esp. 65 ff. For a summary of the traditional position, see Ellis Rivkin, "How Jewish Were the New Christians?" *Hispania Judaica* 2 (1982) 105–15. Noteworthy in this regard is the record of the controversy between Révah and Saraiva, representing respectively the traditionalist and the revisionist positions, that appeared in the literary supplement of the *Diário de Lisboa* in thirteen installments from May 6, 1971 to September 2, 1971, and was reproduced, though imperfectly, in the fifth edition of Saraiva's *Inquisição e Cristãos Novos*. The imperfections have been largely corrected and the lacunae filled in the Salomon-Sassoon translation.

It must not be overlooked that the aforementioned scholars, particularly those in the revisionist camp, often differ significantly amongst themselves, and that these differences, both philosophical and substantive, merit careful analysis in the reformulation of our understanding of the Spanish and Portuguese Inquisitions.

54 The total number of such New Christian refugees can reasonably be put at 30,000. For this see my book, in preparation, *The Marrano Myth: The Inquisition's Weapon Against Modernity*.

55 Martin A. Cohen, ed., *Samuel Usque's Consolation for the Tribulations of Israel* (Philadelphia: Jewish Publication Society of America, 1965; repr. by the Society, 1977) 39.

Report of Tomar itself, in charging that out of the New Christian group came Lutherans and other Christian "heretics" and schismatics, further challenges its own generic assertion of New Christian Judaizing.

Second, that the notorious Judaizing of the New Christians had gotten out of hand. If so, why did the Inquisition wait for the crisis? Certainly it could have moved sooner to counteract the danger.

Obviously such problems do not appear full-blown, like Athena from Zeus' head. The general awareness of the problem implied by the Doctors of Tomar had to be preceded by an awareness on the part of at least some people, whose sense of duty would have impelled them to inform the Inquisition. Does the period of inquisitional quiescence prior to the alleged epidemic of Judaizing indicate that New Christians were successfully deceiving the Inquisition with their religious heresy? Or does it suggest that their Judaizing during the quiescent period was negligible and that the subsequent "explosion" was more figment than fact?

Third, that the Judaizing of the New Christians posed a threat to the faith and security of the Portuguese nation. If so, why did the Pope and the king frequently favor the pretensions of the New Christians? If the purveyors of the myth were correct in imputing New Christian advantages to the power of their subornation, it means that not just the Pope or the king, but the other high officials of both Church and State were also riddled with venality and more concerned with money than the survival of their respective realms. An alternative explanation certainly deserves exploration: namely, that the Papacy and the crown, while understandably not in principle averse to receiving help, were ruled not by money but by concern for their responsibilities; that they did not regard the alleged New Christian threat to be what it was claimed to be; and that their decisions regarding the New Christians were based on religious at least as much as on practical and political criteria.

These and other pointed contradictions were present from the very beginning of the "Marrano myth."[56] Even in the rare periods of intense persecution, the number of documentable Judaizers could not have constituted more than a small fraction of the total New Christian population. Most convicted Judaizers disappeared after their reconciliation. There is no evidence that periods of quiescence were filled with secret Judaizing or devotion to the "ancestral" faith. Despite the alleged dangers of their lack of *limpieza (limpeza) de sangre (sangue)*, New Christians continued to be appointed to important lay and ecclesiastical positions. And throughout the Inquisitorial period, the *conversos'* claim of religious purity received powerful support from high and mighty stations in Old Christian society. The *Sentencia-Estatuto* provoked the anger of the Castilian

---

56 For a more detailed exposition of these inconsistencies, see Cohen, "The Sephardic Phenomenon" 42–47.

king, Juan II, who wanted to punish the city of Toledo for its promulgation. The synods of Alcalá and Vitoria condemned the *Sentencia-Estatuto*. The leading jurist of the day, Alfonso de Montalvo, declared it illegal. In September, 1449, Pope Nicholas V issued a bull denouncing its un-Christian allegations and reiterating the traditional Christian concept of the unity of the faithful. In the following year, he excommunicated those responsible for the *Sentencia-Estatuto*. The *Sentencia-Estatuto* was actively if futilely opposed by the renowned Bishop of Cuenca, Lope de Barrientos. It was also opposed within Toledo's cathedral chapter by men of stature, like the archdeacons of Talavera and Guadalajara, the two sons of the Duke del Infantado, and the illustrious savant, Juan de Vergara. The Catholic piety of the New Christians as a group was regularly defended by notable Old Christians, beginning with Fray Alonso de Oropesa's *Lumen ad revelationem gentium et gloriam plebis tuae Israel* and Juan de Torquemada's *Tractatus contra madianitas et ismaelitas.*[57]

These contradictions can be resolved by transcending the narrow confines of religious argument usually involved in the discussion of the struggle between the Inquisition and the New Christians and focusing on the sociopolitical life of the Iberian Peninsula in the sixteenth and seventeenth centuries.

The salient feature in this panorama is the presence in both Portugal and Spain of a fundamentally regressive aristocracy, resistant to the emergence of modern concepts and institutions. This element was opposed to everything humanistic, liberal, secular and bourgeois. It impeded the development of a middle class beyond a rudimentary stage as well as the forms of rationalized and centralized government which were propelling other colonialist nations of Europe along the road to supremacy in the modern world.[58]

The resistance of the regressive aristocrats was not exclusively or even primarily a struggle of class, as Marxist ideologues frequently claim. Nor were the aristocrats always primarily interested in economic advantage, high though such advantage obviously was on their hierarchy of priorities. While hardly devoid of economic consequences, their struggle, like many another societal struggle, was directed at the consolidation of the power that derived from their ideological position. They and their supporters, whom we shall arbitrarily call the Old Guard, as well as their opponents, whom we shall with equal arbitrariness call the New Guard, both cut sharply across class lines. The Old Guard did

---

57 On the direct defense of the New Christians, see Cohen, *Samuel Usque's Consolation*, 4, 288–89. On the defense of the New Christians in the various early debates over *limpieza de sangre*, see Sicroff *Les controverses*, 36–62.

58 See Francisco Márquez Villanueva, "Los inventos de San Juan de Avila," *Homenaje al Profesor Carriazo* (3 vols.; Seville: Univ. de Sevilla, 1971–73) 3:171–84, esp. 176. The very term "novelty" was regarded as bordering on heresy. See José Antonio Maravall, "La estimación de lo nuevo en la cultura española," *Cuadernos Hispano-americanos*, 171 (1964) 461.

contain the dominant elements of the landed aristocracy and the high echelons of the Iberian Church. But it included as well a preponderant segment of the peasantry. The New Guard contained its share of aristocrats, at first chiefly from the lower echelons of the aristocracy, as well as churchmen and intellectuals, especially the parvenus in their respective hierarchies. These aristocrats "belonged" to the New Guard for a variety of reasons, including the desire for greater wealth and power suggested by the opportunities of the modern world. The New Guard also included merchants, large and small, as well as artisans and craftsmen in cities, towns, and even villages. However, one could expect to find intellectuals and, occasionally, members of the other groups, in the camp of the Old Guard, while the New Guard, judging from the typology of social strife, was not without some participation from other groups, at times doubtless even the peasantry.[59]

These aggregations were not static but dynamic: both individuals and subgroups could and often did try to flow from one position to another on the perennial and ubiquitous spectrum of sociopolitical life. Their movement was conditioned by their changing perceptions of their specific needs and their changing agendas for their satisfaction. These perceptions and agendas reflected the shifting sociopolitical landscapes of Iberian life across the decades and the centuries and the relative positions within these landscapes of the critical institutions of Spain and Portugal, prominent among them the monarchy, the church and the Inquisition. And if at all times there is tension and struggle among the sub-groups of the sociopolitical spectrum, especially those allied with and against the establishment, throughout the period of our consideration the tensions and struggles for power between the constellations of the Old and New Guards were fierce and desperate.[60] While all groups, subgroups and individuals

59 On Portuguese society during this period see especially António Henrique R. de Oliveira Marques, *History of Portugal* (2 vols.; New York: Columbia Univ. Press, 1972) 1:133–216, esp. 178–84. As Oliveira observes (1:490), the study of Portuguese society is hampered by the insufficiency of basic monographs for critical periods, including the closing decades of the fifteenth century. See also Harold Victor Livermore, *A New History of Portugal* (Cambridge, Eng.: Cambridge Univ. Press, [1947] 1976) esp. 163–72 and Stanley G. Payne, *A History of Spain and Portugal* (2 vols.; Madison: Wisconsin, Univ. of Wisconsin Press, 1973) 1:224–45 and 2:390–414. For additional references, see the rich bibliographies of the aforementioned works. The Valencian aristocracy was an exception. Its relationship to the Inquisition is, however, complicated by factors outside the scope of this study. Among these is the considerable initial de facto independence of this aristocracy from the aristocratic power struggling for supremacy at the Castilian court and its eventual subordination to this power. Of the many histories of the Moriscos, see Lea, *The Moriscos of Spain* and Ricardo García Cárcel, *Herejía y sociedad en el siglo XVI: La Inquisición en Valencia 1530–1609* (Barcelona: Ediciones Península, 1980).

60 While the process of "passing over" was more pronounced in Spain in the sixteenth century (e.g., Julio Caro Baroja, *Inquisición, Brujería y criptojudaísmo* (Barcelona: Esplugues de Llobregat, 1970) 30, its incidence in Portugal, particularly beginning with the seventeenth century, was not inconsiderable.

in this struggle for power had their own goals and all carefully surveyed the field to determine which policies might best foster their aims, ultimately everyone was dependent on the ganglia of numbers, wealth and position that endowed the major sub-groups with the potential for dominant power.[61]

The interests of the monarchy lay in concentration of power and rationalized administration. Yet it had to be sensitive to dominant power as well as the strength of its adversaries. In its adamancy and vacillation, it reflected respectively the stability and instability of the dominant power. In its shifts of position, it revealed the administrative options derived from an approximate balance of power.

The New Christians constituted the tonal if not the numerically dominant element of the New Guard. The New Christians did not belong to a single class in Iberian society, but were to be found in nearly all the classes, both New Guard and Old, with the almost certain exception of the peasantry.[62]

They did constitute an important segment, and in some areas, even a majority of the so-called "middle classes," though most of them were professionals, intellectuals, artisans, and petty traders, rather than international merchants, as the Report would have us believe.[63] The Jews who had been expelled from Spain in 1492 and converted by force and fiat in Portugal in 1497 had been similarly positioned. But as non-Christians, Jews lived outside of Christian society and posed no threat to its power elements. The situation of their New Christian descendants was different. As Christians, they possessed a canonical right to full participation in the benefits of Christian society. It was this fact that constituted the threat to the Old Guard, particularly as the New Guard developed in numbers and strength.

It was not in the interest of the Old Guard to destroy the New Guard. If Portugal, like Spain, were to compete against other countries that had entered the modern world, the Old Guard needed the development of "middle class" activities. At the same time it wanted to keep these activities under its control and prevent the New Guard from gaining the power commensurate with the success of New Guard enterprises.[64] Most specifically, this meant blocking the access of

---

61 For a deeper analysis of the sociopolitical dimension of the Inquisition and the alteration of its coordinates at different times and places, see my "The Sephardic Phenomenon."

62 This fact is unmistakably evident from the extant information about identifiable New Christians, especially from inquisitorial trials. For an example of the professional distribution of a group of New Christians tried by a single tribunal, see Haim Beinart, *Records of the Trials of the Spanish Inquisition in Ciudad Real* (4 vols.; Jerusalem: Israel Academy of Sciences and Humanities, 1974–85).

63 For an excellent treatment of the background of this problem see Oliveira Marques, *History of Portugal*, 1:178–90.

64 In my aforementioned study, "The Sephardic Phenomenon," I introduced my term "Modern Old Guard" as a label for the identification of those elements within the Old Guard who exercised this power and therefore the control over the entire polity.

the successful members of the New Guard to the precincts and preserves of the aristocracy, and, simultaneously, blocking the flight of New Christians to more hospitable lands.[65]

A clear reflection of this policy was the presence in Iberia of foreign entrepreneurs, chiefly Italian, French and Dutch, who engaged in major mercantile activities. By the middle of the seventeenth century they numbered nearly 150,000. They constituted approximately two percent of the total Iberian population, but, as outsiders, they posed no threat to Old Guard power. But, as the Old Guard could not have failed to realize, the foreign merchants were only a stopgap and not a solution to their problem.[66] Their loyalty to the Iberian crown was always in question, and their presence did nothing to stop the growth of other segments of the middle classes or the disenchantment of its mercantile elements. Ultimately the indigenous middle classes could not be bypassed without grave danger to the viability of the entire polity. The Old Guard therefore early had to devise ingenious means for controlling their burgeoning power.

The chief means for this control was the "Marrano Myth." Though first appearing in the *Sentencia-Estatuto*, the "Marrano Myth" was probably conceived a quarter century or more earlier. It arose as a direct reaction to the increasingly obvious implications of the large-scale conversion of Jews to Christianity which was taking place at the time. The massive conversions had begun in 1391 in the wake of widespread anti-Jewish disturbances throughout Castile and Aragon, and continued in subsequent decades under the impact of conversionist activities by preachers like the Dominican Vincent Ferrer.[67] The rapid climb on the ladder of success in Spanish life by the converts and their descendants and their alliances in marriage with noble Old Christian families posed a threat to the Old Christians who were, or perceived themselves to be, disadvantaged in this competition. The appearance of the "Marrano Myth" coincided with the rise to prominence of the New Christians.

65 The suppression of the New Christians, their flight and the resultant problems for the Iberian states is recorded in the petition of the New Christians analyzed in the report of Fray Antonio de Soto-mayor to the King Philip on September 17, 1630, in Adler, "Les Marranes d'Espagne et de Portugal," *Revue des Études Juives* 50 (1905) 229–34.

66 On the depletion of the ranks of the New Christian merchants of Spain through their flight after the fall of Olivares and their replacement by foreigners, see also John Lynch, *Spain under the Habsburgs* (2 vols.; New York: Oxford University Press; Oxford: B. Blackwell, 1969) 2:151–52. Clearly, the tonal activity of the New Guard was commerce, especially large-scale commerce. This is dramatically shown in the case of Spain, shortly before the Assembly of Tomar, in the masterly work of Ruth Pike, *Aristocrats and Traders: Sevillian Society in the Sixteenth Century* (Ithaca: Cornell Univ. Press, 1972) esp. 108–9, where Pike emphasizes the importance of the New Christian merchants in the life and power structure of the city.

67 See Baer, *History of the Jews*, 2:166–9. See also Cohen, *Samuel Usque's Consolation*, 194–95. On Vincent Ferrer, see Henri Ghéon, *St. Vincent Ferrer*, F. J. Sheed, trans. (London: Sheed and Ward, 1939) esp. 111–56. See also Pedro M. Cátedra García, *Sermón, Sociedad y Literatura en la Edad Media: San Vicente Ferrer en Castilla (1411–1412): estudio bibliográfico, literario y edición de los textos*

Perhaps the most important fact about the utilization of the myth is that its nuclear concept of blood purity was always selectively applied. When the distinction first appeared, converts and descendants of converts living as Christians in Spain prior to 1391 were declared to be Old Christians, thereby implicitly demonstrating that it was politically possible to neutralize the alleged magnetism of "Jewish blood" to Jewish observance. So, too, in the wake of the general conversion of the Jews in Portugal, King Manuel certified as Old Christians those *conversos* who had been baptized before 1497. But even in the case of the later converts and their descendants, definition in one form or another was able to triumph over blood. Many New Christians resorted to the purchase of spurious genealogies attesting to their Old Christian purity. Others tried to "pass over" by a contrived ignorance of their past. Others still were helped to Old Christian status by acceptance into the high aristocracy.[68] And religious orders often paid little attention to genealogy in the selection and preferment of their members. But in all cases, the ability of New Christians to "pass over" depended upon the kind of work they did, or, perhaps more correctly, the kind of work they did not do. Initially, New Christians engaged in trade, the professions and the urban crafts, could not pass over; they could pass over only if they were involved in activities that did not threaten the Old Guard.[69] By the same token, Old Christians involved in these activities could be regarded as New Christians. As time went on, sociopolitical conditions led to an extension of the boundary of demarcation.[70] By the seventeenth century the entry of New Christians,

---

inéditos (Valladolid, Junta de Castilla y León: Consejería de Cultura y Turismo, 1994).

68 Antonio Domínguez Ortiz, "Los cristianos nuevos: Notas para el estudio de una clase social," *Boletín de la Universidad de Granada* 87 (1949) 251-97.

69 The identification of the entire "middle class" as New Christians (cf. Fréderic Mauro, *Études economiques sur l' expansion portugaise (1500-1900)* (Paris: Centro Cultural Portugais, 1970) 32-54, saying that "la bourgeoisie nouvelle chrétienne pèse d'un poids assez lourd dans la politique et dans l'administration," appears to make the New Christians coterminous with the bourgeoisie. This statement should be modified to include members of the upper classes who were engaged in middle class activities and lower class individuals involved in the support, broadly interpreted, of middle class activities. In other words, the identification of the New Christians must cut across class lines and beyond economic activity in order to include a political dimension. See also p.18. In this connection it is instructive to note that the hostility toward Jews in the literature of Spain was transposed to the New Christians. See, e.g., Miguel Herrero García, *Ideas de los españoles del siglo XVII* (Madrid: Editorial Gredos, 1966) 597-640.

70 The emergence of elements of the New Guard from the nobility or the addition of newcomers of the New Guard from the fifteenth century on led to the separation of the "nobility of blood," limited to Old Christians (and, one might add, almost without exception to the Old Guard) from the nobility proper. For this see Antonio Domínguez Ortiz, *La clase social de los conversos en Castilla en la edad moderna* (Running title: *Los conversos de origen judío después de la expulsión*) (Madrid: Instituto Balmes de Sociología, Departamento de Historia Social, Consejo Superior de Investigaciones Científicas, 1955) 418. The specific references to Old Christian merchants are exceptional and explainable by the continued entry into New Guard activities of Old Christians of established unimpeachable lineage.

especially merchants, into the Old Guard was sufficiently common to be noted in numerous fictional works, especially those written for the theater.[71]

The most striking example of a New Christian who "passed over" is King Ferdinand of Aragon, whose great-grandmother appears to have been a post-1390 convert. As such, she would have transmitted her lack of *limpieza de sangre* to Ferdinand and therefore to all his successors on the throne of Spain and on many another European throne as well.[72]

Correlative to the myth was a body of social values that may appropriately be called the "non-work" ethic. In sharp contrast to the Puritan philosophy evolving elsewhere in contemporary Europe, the "non-work" ethic depreciated commerce and trade and the rest of the broad range of New Guard activity. Its ideal types were the landowner and warrior. It lionized the old nobility and exalted their derivative concept of "honor." Adherence to the "non-work" ethic was the surest way for an individual to enter and remain in the Old Guard. The "non-work"

---

71 As time went on, sociopolitical conditions led to a further extension of the boundary of demarcation. In the seventeenth century the entry of New Christians, especially merchants, into the Old Guard was sufficiently common to be noted in fictional works, especially those written for the theater. See, for example, Antonie Adrianus Van Beysterveldt, *Repercussions du souci de la pureté de sang sur la conception de 'honneur, dans la "comedia nueva" espagnole* (Leiden: E. J. Brill, 1966) 185 ff.

72 Ferdinand's mother, Juana Enríquez, was a granddaughter of María Hernández, known as the "Paloma de [Dove of] Toledo." See Meyer (Moritz) Kayserling's still valuable article, "Ferdinand and Isabella," *The Jewish Encyclopedia* (12 vols.; New York: Funk and Wagnalls Company) 5:363–64 and the bibliography contained therein. David Romano, in a valuable study, "¿Ascendencia judía de Fernando el Católico?" *Sefarad* 55 (1995) 163–72 questions the validity of the attribution of Jewish ancestry to King Ferdinand. He correctly records that the information regarding Ferdinand's Jewish ancestry is scant and insufficiently precise. But there is little hope of finding stronger corroborative documentation from contemporary sources, if for no other reason than the fact that beginning with the massive conversions in Aragon in 1391 it would have been indiscreet, if indeed not dangerous, for individuals to flaunt their Jewish ancestry, and for enemies of powerful families with such ancestry to publish such information. Given the fact that the large percentage of Aragonese Jewry converted in the late fourteenth and fifteenth centuries and that widespread intermarriage ensued between New and Old Christians, especially Old Christians in the upper echelons of society, throughout the fifteenth century, it would not be appropriate to dismiss the presumption regarding Ferdinand's Jewish ancestry, let alone deny its likelihood, pending the emergence of incontrovertible evidence. The widespread mingling of New Christian and Old Christian lines is obliquely attested in the Green Book of Aragon (*El Libro Verde de Aragón*) compiled most probably at the end of the fifteenth century, but certainly no later than the first lustrum of the sixteenth, ostensibly to inform Old Christians interested in maintaining their blood purity about the Jewish ancestry of their prospective in-laws. See Juan de Anchías, fl. 1507 *[El] Libro Verde de Aragón: Documentos Aragoneses*, Isidro de las Cagigas, ed. (Madrid: Compañia Ibero-Americana de Publicaciones, 1929) 14 and passim. The mingling of Old Christians and New Christians is also attested by the distinguished Jesuit, Diogo de Areda, who in the early third decade of the seventeenth century stated explicitly that "there is no family of importance in which there are not many men and women who share Jewish blood." Areda, *Discurso Jurídico Político* Ms. Biblioteca Nacional, Cod. 8702, fundo antigo, cited by Azevedo, *Cristãos Novos*, 214. See also the *Discurso* itself, fol. 8b–9a.

ethic thus possessed an obvious connection to the concept of *limpieza de sangre/ limpeza de sangue.*

The connection of the two concepts was additionally utilized to channel the resentment of the disadvantaged and oppressed echelons of Spanish and Portuguese society. These groups were known to be almost, if not entirely, free of "Jewish blood," for the simple reason that few Jews had found it desirable to marry into their ranks. If there had been any unfortunate enough to do so, it is most likely that they were quickly absorbed and their Jewish roots forgotten long before Jewish origins became a problem for Iberian society. At the same time, if these groups were occupationally involved, it was nowhere in the realm of New Guard activity.

The Old Guard exalted these people's purity of blood and the nobility of their occupations, however lowly these might have been. It even exalted their often enforced idleness as preferable to the work of the New Guard. It thereby sought to instill a pride of race and a satisfaction with their condition that narcotized them against the changing society and displaced their hostility on the "Jewish merchants" of the New Guard.

It is thus clear that from the very beginning, the determining factor in distinguishing New Christians from Old was less the touted concept of blood cleanness than a pedestrian and pragmatic sociopolitical consideration.

The Marrano Myth was thus instrumental in creating two distinct or, at least when needed, distinguishable societies in the Iberian Peninsula and its possessions. One of these was an in-caste of dominant power, the other an out-caste, contoured along arbitrary ethnic and ethno-religious lines, whose state of grace was not unrelated to the in-caste's perception of its own security. The out-castes were indiscriminately called Jews, in either a religious or an ethnic sense, and deprecated as "foreigners" in contrast to the in-caste's "native Portuguese."[73]

The Holy Office of the Inquisition was the implement of the Marrano Myth. It was introduced into Castile in 1480, Aragon in 1484 and Portugal a little more than a half century later.[74] The ostensible purpose of the Inquisition was to

---

73 See Van Beysterveldt, *Repercussions.*

74 On the Inquisition and the myth see, inter alia, António Nunes Ribeiro Sanches [1699–1783] *Origem da denominacão de christão velho e christão novo em Portugal* (written between 1735 and 1748 and remained in manuscript), first edition by Raul Rêgo (Lisbon: publisher not listed, 1956) and *Christãos Novos e Christãos Velhos em Portugal,* Raul Rêgo, ed. (Lisbon: Paisagem, 1973) and second edition, Porto, Paisagem (sic), 1973 (sic); António Baião, "O sangue infecto do Pe. António Vieira," *O Instituto* 77 (Coimbra, 1929) 1–10; Edouard Roditi, "O fábrico de judeus ou a Inquisição em Portugal," *Occidente, Nova serie,* 399 (Lisbon: July, 1971) (40)–47; and Francisco Bethencourt, "A Inquisição," in Yvette Kace Centeno, *Portugal. Os Mitos Revisitados* (Lisbon: Edições Salamandra, 1993) 99–138. The racist myth provides the basis for Mario Sá's *A invasão dos judeus* (Lisbon: Imprensa L. da Silva, 1925). Of interest also is Elias Lipiner's essay, "O cristão-novo: mito ou realidade," in Yosef Kaplan, *Jews and Conversos: Studies in Society and the Inquisition* (Jerusalem: World Union of Jewish Studies, Magnes Press, 1985) 124–38. See also, more generally, Raphael and Jennifer Patai, *The Myth*

prosecute heresy, particularly among Judaizing New Christians. Gauged by the declarations of the Old Guard and echoed in the Marrano Myth, the successes in this mission were modest and unenduring. But in the psychological area the Inquisition's achievement was phenomenal. Every one of its arrests sent shock waves of terror through the entire circle of the prisoner's acquaintances and friends. They worried whether they were already marked for arrest for crimes they had committed or might be falsely accused of committing or whether they would be denounced, even falsely, by the prisoner during the Inquisition's secret trial. A dozen arrests could thus conceivably terrorize a significant segment of the entire New Christian community.

There can be no question that the Inquisition's greatest effectiveness was as an instrument of intimidation. It riddled all New Christians with insecurity, regardless of position, class or Catholic piety. In so doing, it was especially able to keep the middle class, or, more correctly, the entire New Guard, reasonably in check in accordance with the general policy of the Old Guard.[75] It could thus

---

of the Jewish Race ([New York: Scribner's, 1975] Detroit: Wayne State Univ. Press, 1989). Especially noteworthy here is the use of the racial mythology by Nazi Germany (see esp. the notes on 406).

75 On the introduction of the Inquistion, see Lea, *History of the Inquisition*, 1:147, 160–227; Herculano, *Inquisição em Portugal*; and Benzion Netanyahu, *The Origins of the Inquisition in Fifteenth Century Spain* (New York: Random House, 1995). Among the important related works on the Inquisition see António Baião, *A Inquisição em Portugal e no Brasil: Subsídios para a sua História* (3 vols.; Lisbon:[publisher not listed], [1906] 1921); João Lúcio Azevedo, "Os processos da Inquisição como documentos de História," *Boletim da Classe de Letras [da] Academia das Sciências de Lisboa* 13 (3) (Lisbon, 1919) (1004)–1028, and, by the same title in *Memórias da Academia das Ciências de Lisboa. Classe de Letras* 1 (Lisbon, 1935) (67)–85; also his *Cristãos Novos*. See also Baião's classic work, *Episódios dramáticos da Inquisição Portugesa* (Porto: Edição da Renascença, 1919; 2d ed., 3 vols.; Lisbon: Seara Nova, 1936–38); Israel Salvator Révah, *Études Portugaises* (Paris: Fundação Calouste Gulbenkian, Centro Cultural Portugues, 1975); Sonia A. Siqueira, *A Inquisição portuguesa e a sociedade colonial*, 115–312, and Francisco Bethencourt, *L'Inquisition à l'époque moderne: Espagne, Portugal, Italie XVe–XIXe siècle* (Paris: Fayard, 1995); See also Saraiva, *Inquisição e Cristãos Novos*; María José Pimenta Ferro Tavares, *Os Judeus em Portugal no século XV* (2 vols.; Lisbon: Univ. Nova de Lisboa, Faculdade de Ciências Sociais e Humanas, 1982–84), esp. the charts on the *conversos* in 2:870–907; her *Judaismo e Inquisição* (Lisbon: Editorial Presença, 1987); and the following collections: Joaquín Pérez Villanueva and Bartolomé Escandell Bonet, eds., *Historia de la Inquisición en España y América*, Biblioteca de Autores Cristianos (2 vols.; Madrid: Centro de Estudios Inquisitoriales, 1984–93); the earlier volume edited by Pérez Villanueva, *La Inquisición española: nueva visión, nuevos horizontes* (Madrid: Siglo Veintiuno de España, 1980); Angel Alcalá, ed., *Inquisición española y mentalidad inquisitorial* (Barcelona: Ariel, 1984), translated as *The Spanish Inquisition and the Inquisitorial Mind* (Boulder, Colorado: Social Science Monographs and Highland Lakes, New Jersey: Atlantic Research and Publications, Distributed by Columbia Univ. Press, New York, 1987); the important collection in Gustav Henningsen and John Tedeschi, eds., in association with Charles Amiel, *The Inquisition in Early Modern Europe: Studies on Sources and Methods* (De Kalb, Illinois: Northern Illinois Univ. Press, 1986), esp. the studies entitled "The Archives and Historiography of the Spanish Inquisition" (pp. 54–78) by Henningsen, translated by Lawrence Scott Rainey, and "The Archives of the Portuguese Inquisition: A Brief Survey" (pp. 79–99) by Charles Amiel, also translated by Rainey; and Stephen Haliczer, *Inquisition and Society*

even control the most important banking families without the commercially counterproductive incarcerations of their members. It could also similarly move to repress any intellectuals whose ideas or positions it regarded as incompatible with the best interests of the Old Guard.

By thus intimidating all New Christians the Old Guard could control the modernizing elements of society in which the New Christians played a significant if not dominant role. It could likewise control the pre-modern divisions of society in which anyone descended from a convert, or in a position to be so presumed, could be regarded as potentially dangerous. The dossiers of the Inquisition leave no doubt that "pure-blooded" Old Christians were in danger of apprehension by the Inquisition in direct ratio to their involvement in the intellectual, commercial or political activities of the New Guard.[76] These dos-

---

in *Early Modern Europe* (London: Croom Helm, 1987) 47–63.

76 See Henry Kamen, *The Spanish Inquisition: A Historical Revision* (New Haven: Yale Univ. Press, 1998) 239; Israel Salvator Révah, "Les marranes portugais et l'Inquisition au xvie siècle," in Richard D. Barnett, ed., *The Sephardi Heritage: Essays on the Historical and Cultural Contribution of the Jews of Spain and Portugal* (2 vols.; London: Valentine Mitchell, 1971–89) 1:479–526. On the racial dimension, see Netanyahu's, *Origins of the Inquisition*, particularly his section on "The Origins of the Inquisition," 925–1092 and his discussion of "Old Christian Apologies for the Conversos," 606–27. See also Netanyahu, "On the Historical Meaning of the Hebrew Sources Related to the Marranos (A Reply to Critics)," *Hispania Judaica* 1 (1980) 77–102. Regarding the confessions of Judaism by Old Christians, confessions whose sincerity could be put to question, see also the interesting memorial, known as the *Notícias Recônditas do Modo de Proceder a Inquisição de Portugal com os seus Prezos* ever since the appearance of its third and expanded edition in Lisbon in 1821. The original Portuguese version, a translation of a tract in English originally titled *An Account of the Cruelties Exercised by the Inquisition in Portugal* (London, 1708), was included in a work in Spanish published in Vila Franca (i.e., London) in 1722 and entitled *Notícias Recónditas y Pósthumas de las Inquisiciones de España y Portugal con sus Presos*. From the time of the second Portuguese edition, in Venice, 1750, the work has often been incorrectly attributed to Father António Vieira. It is included in his *Obras escolhidas do Pe António Vieira*, António Sérgio and Hernâni Cidade, eds. (12 vols.; Lisbon: Livraria Sá da Costa, 1951–54) 4:139–244. See esp. 224–25 and the case of Afonso Nobre of Vila Viçosa on 221.

    Henry Kamen correctly points out that in Spain the doctrine of limpieza "had a restricted impact and was often scorned by the social and intellectual elite, and did not have much effect among the mass of the population." "Limpieza and the Ghost of Americo Castro: Racism as a Tool of Literary Analysis," *Hispanic Review* 64 (1966) 27. Of course, the restricted *impact* of the concept was its pars pro toto sociopolitical use against the New Guard. This, perhaps more than any other reason, explains why the majority of the New Christian population remained immune to its application, and why those who knew what was going on could, within the perimeters of licitness, express their scorn for the concept. Essentially, for all the differences in situational details, the same analysis applies to Portugal.

    Certainly one of the most exemplary cases of such application in the Iberian Peninsula was the prosecution of Fray Luis de León (1528 [1527?]–91). Fray Luis was unquestionably of Jewish descent, but he was certainly not involved in Jewish practice, as charged by the indictment against him. He was, however, a man of intellectual stature and independence. Of the vast literature on this subject, see, inter alia, Humberto Pinera, *El pensamiento español de los siglos xvi y xvii* (New York; Las Américas, 1970) 93–147.

siers also reveal the extent of the Inquisition's pursuit of liberal and humanistic thought through the creation of a psychologically repressive atmosphere, not the least dimension of which was the Damoclean threat of criminal prosecution.[77]

77 On humanism, see, inter alia, Elisabeth Feist Hirsch, *Damião de Goes: The Life and Thought of a Portuguese Humanist 1502-1574* (The Hague: M. Nijhoff, 1967) 129-90. António José Teixeira. *António Homem e a Inquisição* (Coimbra: Imprensa da Univ., 1895-1902) 11-25 and passim; see also the *Notícias recônditas* in the *Obras escolhidas do Pe António Vieira* (see n. 75 above), passim; Enrique Llamas Martínez, "Sequelas de la acción de la Inquisición española contra los libros de la Madre Teresa de Jesús (1593-1607)," *Cultura: História e filosofia* 5 (1986) 289-317; Maria do Rosário de Sampaio Themudo Barata de Azevedo Cruz, "António Ferreira e o humanismo jurídico," *Cultura: História e filosofia* 5 (1986) 735-49; Américo da Costa Ramalho, *Estudos sobre a época do Renascimento* (Coimbra: Instituto de Alta Cultura, 1969); his *Estudos sobre o século XVI* (Paris: Centro Cultural Portugues, 1980) with its excellent introduction, 1-20 and the splendid volume by Luis de Albuquerque, et al., *L'Humanisme Portugais et l'Europe: Actes du XXIe Colloque International d'Études Humanistes,* Jean-Claude Margolin and José V. de Pina Martins, eds. (Paris: Fundação Calouste Gulbenkian, Centro Cultural Portugues, 1984).

Intimately connected with humanism was the panoply of thought that was collected under the umbrella designation of Erasmianism. This thought included many strands that were directly influenced by Desiderius Erasmus (1466?-1536) and many others that were at least as much influenced by the broader atmosphere of the liberal and humanistic thought of his and subsequent generations. In the Iberian Peninsula, as elsewhere, the direct relationship of this thought to the sociopolitical position of the New Guard cannot be overemphasized, but this aspect, too, is beyond the scope of the present study. For our purposes suffice it to cite the classical work of Marcel Bataillon, *Érasme et l'Espagne: recherches sur l'histoire spirituelle du XVIe siècle* (Paris: E. Droz, 1937) and four works specific to Portugal: António José Saraiva, *Para a História da cultura em Portugal* (Lisbon: Centro Bibliográfico, 1946); José V. de Pina Martins, *Humanismo e Erasmismo na cultura portuguesa do século XVI* (Paris: Fundação Calouste Gulbenkian, Centro Cultural Portugues, 1973); Artur Moreira de Sá, *De re erasmiana: aspectos do erasmismo na cultura portuguesa do século XVI* (Braga: Univ. de Lisboa, Faculdade de Filosofia, 1977) and José V. de Pina Martins, et al., eds., *O Humanismo Português 1500-1600: primeiro simpósio nacional* (Lisbon: Academia das Ciências de Lisboa, 1988).

For a classical example of the pursuit of liberal and humanistic thinking under the rubric of Erasmianism, see João Sebastião da Silva Dias, *O Erasmismo e a Inquisição em Portugal: O processo [1560-62] de Fr. Valentim da Luz* (Coimbra: Univ. of Coimbra, 1975) with a transcript of the trial and an excellent introduction, 1-64. See esp. 34-53.

On censorship as a form of social control see Francisco Bethencourt, "Inquisição e controle social," *História Crítica* 14 (1987) 13-31; António Baião, "A censura literária da Inquisição no século XVII — subsídios para a sua história," *Boletim da Segunda Classe da Academia das Ciências de Lisboa* 9 (1915) 356-79, and his, "A censura literária inquisitorial," 12 (1917-18) 473-560. See also Alvaro Huerga, *Historia de los alumbrados, 1570-1630* (4 vols.; Madrid: Fundación Univ. Española, Seminario Cisneros, 1978-94), passim; Virgilio Pinto Crespo, *Inquisición y control ideológico en la España del siglo XVI* (Madrid: Taurus, 1983) and his study, "Institucionalización inquisitorial y censura de libros," in Pérez Villanueva, *La Inquisición española,* 513-36, esp. 516, "De manera más específica podemos afirmar que la actividad censorial fué un instrumento al servicio del control de la producción y de la difusión ideológicas"; Sicroff, *Les controverses;* and three studies by José Veiga Torres: "Uma longa guerra social: os ritmos da repressão inquisitorial em Portugal," *Revista de História Económica e Social* 1 (1978) 55-68; "Uma longua (sic) guerra social: Novas perspectivas para o estudo da Inquisição portuguesa — A Inquisição de Coimbra," *Revista da História das Ideias*

So do dramatically the inquisitional indexes of forbidden books.[78] The sociopolitical conception and application of the concept of blood purity is nowhere
better evidenced than in a telling statement, possibly echoing a popular proverb:
"In their blood New Christians have sin, Old Christians the remedy."[79]

---

8 (1986) 56–70; and "Da repressão religiosa para a promoção social. A Inquisição como instância
legitimadora da promoção social da burguesia comercial," *Revista crítica das ciências sociais* 40
(1994) 109–35. See also Yvonne Cunha Rego, ed., *Feiticeiros, profetas e visionários: textos antigos
portugueses* (Lisbon: Imprensa Nacional, Casa da Moeda, Biblioteca Nacional, 1981), and António
José Saraiva, *A política de discriminação social e a repressão da heterodoxia* (Lisbon: Jornal do Foro,
1958). See also his *História da cultura em Portugal* and Novinski, "Sistema de poder e repressão
religiosa." Of the innumerable pertinent comparisons in other societies, see, as an interesting
example, the study by Helio Oswaldo Alves, "Restrições à liberdade da imprensa numa sociedade
de direito: A Inglaterra em 1819," *Diacrítica* 11 (1996) 245–65. See also Bartolomé Escandell, "La
Inquisición como dispositivo de control social y la pervivencia actual del 'modelo inquisitorial,'"
in Angel Alcalá, et al., eds., *Inquisición española y mentalidad inquisitorial* (Barcelona: Ariel, 1984)
597–611. Escandell points out, however, that the Inquisition had existed in other places before its
introduction into Castile, "and that, in inquisitorial material, Spain has invented nothing which
had not already been applied in other countries and places," 599. It is, however, important to keep
in mind some of the fundamental distinctions between the Spanish and Portuguese Inquisitions.
On the Inquisition as an instrument of societal control, see the excellent contribution of Virgilio
Pinto Crespo, "La censura: Sistemas de control e instrumentos de acción" in Alcalá, *Inquisicion*,
269–87 and Angel Alcalá, "Control inquisitorial de humanistas y escritores," 288–314.

78 On the Indexes, see Fr. Heinrich Rausch, *Die Indices Librorum Prohibitorum des sechzehnten Jahr-
hunderts* (Tübingen: Litterarischen Verein in Stuttgart, 1886); Artur Moreira de Sá, ed., *Indices dos
livros proibidos em Portugal no século* XVI (Lisbon: Instituto Nacional de Investigação Científica,
1983); Jesús Martínez de Bujanda, ed., with the assistance of René Davignon and Ela Stanek,
Index de L'Inquisition espagnole: 1551, 1554, 1559 (Sherbrooke, Quebec: Centre d'Études de la
Renaissance, l'Univ. de Sherbrooke, 1984); Jesús Martínez de Bujanda, ed., with the assistance of
René Davignon and Ela Stanek, and with a historical introduction by Leon E. Halkin, *Index de
l'Université de Louvain: 1546, 1550, 1558* (Sherbrooke, Quebec: Centre d'Études de la Renaissance,
l'Univ. de Sherbrooke, 1986); Jesús Martínez de Bujanda, ed., with the assistance of René Davignon
and Ela Stanek, and with a historical introduction by Paul F. Grendler translated by Claude Sutto,
Index de Venise, 1549; Venise et Milan, 1554 (Sherbrooke, Quebec: Centre d'Études de la Renaissance,
l'Univ. de Sherbrooke, 1987); Jesús Martínez de Bujanda, ed., with the assistance of René Davignon,
Ela Stanek and Marcella Richter, *Thesaurus de la littérature interdite au* XVIe *siècle* (Sherbrooke,
Quebec: Centre d'Études de la Renaissance, l'Univ. de Sherbrooke, 1996); Anne Sauvy, with an
introductory study by Motoko Ninomiya, *Livres saisis à Paris entre 1678 et 1701* (The Hague: M.
Nijhoff, 1972); and Gabriel Peignot, *Dictionnaire critique, littéraire et bibliographique des principaux
livres condamnés au feu, supprimés ou censurés* (2 vols.; Paris: A. A. Renouard, 1806).

For background studies, see Israel Salvator Révah, *La censure inquisitoriale portugaise au* XVIe
siècle (Lisbon: Instituto de Alta Cultura, 1960) and Angel Alcalá, "La censura inquisitorial de la
literatura del Siglo de Oro en España y en Portugal: Comparacion de sus 'Indices' y sus resultados,"
in Gilberto Huber and Ferdinando Bastos de Souza, eds., *Inquisição: Ensaios sobre mentalidade,
heresias e arte: trabalhos apresentados no I Congresso Internacional "Inquisição," Universidade de
São Paolo, Maio 1987, organizadoras Anita Novinsky e María Luiza Tucci Carneiro* (Rio de Janeiro:
Expressão e Cultura; São Paolo: EDUSP, 1992) 421–36.

79 See *Notícias Recônditas* in Vieira, *Obras Escolhidas*, 4:227.

While it had no choice but to prosecute overt cases of Judaizing whose unquestionable notoriety challenged its authority and credibility, the Inquisition could pick and choose as it saw fit among the doubtful or "secret" Judaizers, real or imagined. Its depopulation in the early seventeenth century of selected Portuguese villages containing large numbers of New Christians serves as an apt example of its methods of intimidation.[80] The fright that these actions engendered in the totality of the New Christian community is evidenced by repeated references in New Christian petitions for the curbing of inquisitional power.[81]

All of this reinforces the startling conclusion that the functional distinction between Old Christians and New Christians derived not primarily from religion or ethnicity, but from sociopolitical position. It removes all doubt that the concept of blood purity was sociopolitically conceived and sociopolitically applied.[82] Through its application the Inquisition wielded the awesome authority to determine who among Portugal's huge New Christian population could or could not "pass over" to the Old Christian side.[83] The Inquisition, also, of course,

80 Adler, "Les Marranes d'Espagne et de Portugal," *Revue des Études Juives* 50 (1905) 230. Cf. Azevedo, *Cristãos Novos*, 334–36. The deserted village syndrome continued to plague Portugal throughout the period of the Inquisition, as was noted by the distinguished eighteenth century diplomat Luiz da Cunha (d. 1749), a former confidant of Kings Pedro II (regent 1668–83, king 1683–1706) and João V (1706–50), and Portuguese ambassador to Vienna, the Hague and Paris. In his *Testamento Político* (Lisbon: Impressão Régia, 1820), addressed to the prince José before his ascent to the throne as José I (1750–77), he details the extent of the desolation: "Da mesma sorte dissera que V. A. acharía certas boas povoações quasi desertas, como por exemplo na Beira Alta, os grandes lugares de Covilhã, Fundão e Cidade da Guarda, e de Lamego; em Trás os Montes, a Cidade de Bragança; e destruidas as suas manifacturas. E se V.A. preguntar a causa desta dissolução, não sei se alguma pessoa se atreverá a dizer-lha com a liberdade que eu terei a honra de fazello, e vem a ser que a Inquisição prendendo hum por crime do Judaismo e fazendo fugir outros para fora do Reino com os seus cabedaes, por temerem que lhos confiscassem se fossem prezos, foi preciso que as taes manifacturas cahissem, porque os chamados Christãos novos os sustentavão, e os seus obreiros, que nellas trabalhavão, eram em grande número, foi necessario que se espalhassem, e fossem viver em outras partes e tomassem outros officios para ganharem o seu pão, porque ninguem se quiz deixar morrer de fame" (p. 37). See also the Report, f. 83a.

81 See for example, Azevedo, *Cristãos Novos*, 149–50. Cf. Adler, "Les Marranes d'Espagne et de Portugal," *Revue des Études Juives* 51 (1906) 97–98, leading to the Junta that articulated the fourteen points that are discussed in the body of the text below.

82 For a precious glimpse into the political utilization of religious ideology against the New Christians, see Juan (sic) Martins de Lassao, "*Documento sobre os Cristãos Novos mandado ao inquisidor geral de Espanha, August 19, 1527*," transcribed by M. L. E. (Maria Luísa Esteves) in A. da Silva Rego, ed., *As Gavetas da Torre do Tombo* (12 vols.; Lisbon: Centro de Estudos Históricos Ultramarinos, 1960–77) 1 (Gavetas I–II):103–24.

83 On the other hand, individuals of obvious New Christian descent, even with emigré parents who adopted Judaism, could be elevated to positions of Old Guard status. One of the most interesting of such cases is that of Bishop Francisco de Victoria (1540–92), the first bishop in the South American territory that is now Argentina and, according to Jonathan I. Israel, possibly the only Portuguese New Christian to be elevated to a bishopric in the sixteenth century. Jonathan I. Israel,

possessed the authority to determine which of the New Christians to prosecute and when. If the suggestions of the Report were implemented the Inquisition would also ultimately hold the Damoclean threat of expulsion over the heads of all people it (or the power behind it) chose to regard as New Christians.

Naturally connected with this creation of Old Christians and exposure of New Christians is the frequently posed question of whether the Inquisition actually created secret Judaizers in the discharge of its functions. The answer to this question is quite complex. On the one hand, there can be little doubt that many New Christians chose a Jewish identification both in the years immediately following the massive conversions in Aragon and Castile in the last decade of the fourteenth century and in Portugal at the end of the fifteenth, and in the decades and centuries that followed these events. Their choice stemmed from many factors, ranging from a rejection of the conversion by the initial converts or their descendants to personal epiphanies and situational pressures, but of the voluntary nature of such elections there can be no doubt. Nor can there be any doubt that such individuals would have sought to indoctrinate, and, as is shown in incontestable evidence, did in fact indoctrinate their children and others into beliefs and practices that would define them as Jews. Furthermore, in the wake of these massive conversions it was inevitable for some or many New Christians who accepted their conversions to continue some Jewish practices and customs, out of habit, and that such practices and customs persisted in both Spain and Portugal and their respective colonies for decades and even centuries, even if in diminished numbers and attenuated and often corrupted form, and even if increasingly devoid of Jewish content and any memory of Jewish origins. On the other hand, an abundance of data suggests that fear helped to create admissions of Judaizing by numerous defendants in inquisitional trials who may or may not have been practicing Judaism clandestinely but who knew that their admission of so doing could bring them reconciliation with the Church. So did false evidence and torture during the inquisitional process. While it is impossible to know how many of these presumptive secret Judaizers had not been actual secret Judaizers prior to their arrest but became actual secret Judaizers during the ordeals associated with their trials, it is possible to identify at least some New Christians who belong to this category. Having been rejected by the instruments of the faith into which they had been baptized, in which they were reared and on which in many cases they had bestowed their zealous devotion, they took refuge in Judaism, or, more precisely, the Judaism as they understood it to be and were

---

"Duarte Nunes da Costa (Jacob Curiel) of Hamburg, Sephardi Nobleman and Communal Leader (1585–1664)," *Studia Rosenthaliano* 21 (1986/1987) 15. See also Francisca Vendrell, "Concesión de nobleza a un converso," *Sefarad* 8 (1948) 397–401. The article deals with the converso Samuel Najari, who was baptized and took the name Gil Ruiz Najari at the beginning of 1416. He was ennobled by King Don Fernando de Antequera.

or were presumed to be following, and sought the bonding companionship of other New Christians who found themselves similarly positioned.

In this connection, it should be stated that the emergence of New Christians as Jews in the Portuguese Diaspora and the development of authentic Jewish communities out of former New Christians in no way demonstrates that they had in each instance identified as Jews in the Peninsula. This phenomenon was largely conditioned by the circumstances of the Portuguese New Christian diaspora.[84]

The reliance on religion as the vehicle of discrimination is explainable on the ground that the Catholic faith formed the strongest unifying force in the society of that time. It was one of the few ideologies for which the common folk could confidently have been expected to fight and die. It possessed two additional useful features: On the one hand it was strongly entrenched in the pre-modern way of life and was intimately connected with Old Guard power. On the other, in the Jew, it could provide a historically rooted "Enemy," with sufficient affect to magnetize hostility and galvanize it to action. It mattered little to Portugal's Old Guard, as it did to earlier purveyors of the myth, that many New Christians were religiously not Jewish at all; that many, certainly the vast majority by the beginning of the seventeenth century, had few Jews in their ancestry, and that often these ancestral Jews were many generations removed. Like every other revelation of a common "Enemy," an archconservative Old Guard could balloon the objectionable characteristics of a few or the imaginary characteristics of a group into a generic accusation.[85]

84 David Franco Mendes, *Memorias do estabelecimento e progresso dos judeus Portuguezes e espanhoes nesta famosa citade de Amsterdam* [up to 1772] edited by Lajb Fuks and R.G. Fuks-Mansfeld, with a philological commentary, analysis and glossary by Benjamin Nicolaas Teensma, *Studia Rosenthaliano* 9:2 (1975) i-xii and 1–204. See also Yosef Haim Yerushalmi, "Conversos Returning to Judaism in the 17th Century: Their Jewish Knowledge and Psychological Readiness" (Heb.), *Proceedings of the Fifth World Congress of Jewish Studies*, 2 (1969) 201–209. One of the finest examples of commitment to Judaism is to be found in the case of Luis de Carvajal, the Younger, who at a critical juncture of his life chose the path of Judaism and ultimately the road to martyrdom. For this see Martin A. Cohen, *The Martyr* (Philadelphia: Jewish Publication Society of America, 1973. 2d ed.; Albuquerque, New Mexico: Univ. of N. Mex. Press, 2001).

85 On this aspect see Cohen, "Toward a New Comprehension . . ." concluding section. The identification of the New Christians, regarded generically as Judaizers, with the New Guard, is evident from the anti-New Christian records of many works. See, for example, the fascinating tract by Miguel (Michele) Soriano (Suriano), *Relatione di Portogallo et sua Historia et principio dell'Inquisitione . . .* Ms. Biblioteca Nacional (Madrid), no. 763, fols. 118a–26, esp. 118b. The tract was composed not long after King Sebastian's disastrous defeat at Alcazarquivir in 1578. For the traditional anti-New Christian polemic, see Edward Glaser, "Invitation to Intolerance. A Study of Portuguese Sermons Preached at Autos-da-Fé," *HUCA* 27 (1956) 327–85. See also, Israel Salvator Révah, "Le Plaidoyer en faveur des 'nouveaux-Chrétiens' portugais du licencié Martín González de Cellorigo (Madrid, 1619)" *Revue des Études Juives – Historia Judaica* 2 (122) (1963) 279–398. Interested in the "natural laws" of economics and society, Cellorigo opines that many New Christians are sincere Catholics and seeks more equitable treatment for them. See 197, 324 and passim.

The recognition of a basal political role for the Portuguese and, indeed, all the Iberian Inquisitions, casts the long controversy over the New Christians' religiosity in a startlingly new light. It provides a more consistent and coherent explanation than any other hitherto suggested as to why some reputable Christian leaders claimed that New Christian Judaizing constituted a danger to the state and demanded some form of ostracism for the culpable caste, while others no less devout did not regard it as a problem of magnitude, if a problem at all, and insisted on the removal of all obstacles to the New Christians' integration into society. It explains why, despite all the cries of danger from their opponents, New Christians continued to be appointed to positions of trust and honor by the highest echelons of society, including the crown. It explains above all why the Inquisition, which resonated and reverberated the claim of pandemic Iberian Judaizing, prosecuted only a minuscule percentage of the New Christians and sent only a fraction of these to condemnation.

The positing of a political role for the Inquisition should not lead to the erroneous assumption that it was unconcerned with matters of faith. The Iberian Inquisition, of course, inherited the traditional inquisitorial concern with a variety of crimes against the Catholic faith that had nothing to do with Judaism. To this category belonged cases involving blasphemy, bigamy, concubinage and solicitation in the confessional. It also had to be concerned with notorious expressions of Judaism that challenged its authority and credibility even if they had nothing to do with its political aims. At times such overt devotion to Judaism came from New Christians whose position in society might otherwise have permitted them to pass over to the Old Christian side. On other occasions they came from Old Christians. Yet, for all this complexity, the records of the Inquisition leave no doubt that, at least until the time of the Assembly of Tomar, it concentrated principally on people located in the area broadly definable as the New Guard.

Its multidimensional responsibilities help to explain why, contrary to popular belief, the Inquisition was never exclusively or even primarily dedicated to the prosecution of the wealthy. Although in some periods, as at the beginning of its activity in Castile, the victims included large numbers of well-heeled New Christian citizens, the Inquisition just as often prosecuted the lowly and the poor. In the seventeenth century, it chronically tottered on the brink of bankruptcy.[86] Economically as well as politically, it was subordinated to the crown and through the crown to the Old Guard.

By the beginning of the second quarter of the seventeenth century, the problem of the Portuguese Old Guard had reached the crisis point. Their nation was in the throes of decline. Already apparent by the middle of the sixteenth century, the decline had accelerated after the union of Portugal with Spain in 1580 as a

---

86 On the poverty of the Inquisition, see Lea, *History of the Inquisition*, 2:433–45.

result of the policies of the Castilian monarchs who ruled both countries from Madrid. At the time of the Assembly of Tomar, Portugal was seething with discontent. It was militarily weak, economically impoverished, and psychologically dispirited. Its Old Guard leadership saw its position threatened as it had never been before.[87]

In the eyes of the Portuguese, the three Spanish kings, all named Philip, who had ruled Portugal since its union with Spain, all contributed to its problems. Under Felipe II of Spain (1556–98), who ruled Portugal as Filipe I (1580–98), Portugal lost most of the thirty-one ships it had contributed to the ill-fated Armada of 1588. Under Felipe III (1598–1621), known as Filipe II of Portugal, it witnessed Madrid pushing the Iberian Empire into the Thirty Years War in order to protect Spain's Netherlands and a land lifeline to its possessions in Italy. Under Felipe IV of Spain (1621–65) who ruled as Filipe III of Portugal (1621–40), it became the adversary of England, which declared war on Spain in 1625 and France, which three years later began a struggle to divest it of the Duchy of Mantua.

Nor did Spain's hostility with Holland help the Portuguese cause. In 1619, after a ten year truce with Spain, the Dutch dealt the Spanish fleet a crippling blow which in effect spelled the end of its supremacy among the European powers. It then stepped up its attacks on the outposts of the Portuguese Empire, in both the Far East and the Americas. Particularly disheartening to the Portuguese was the Dutch seizure of the port of Bahia in Brazil in 1624. Although Madrid did help to rout the Dutch the following year, it could not deploy sufficient forces to prevent a more permanent Dutch foothold from being established at Recife in 1630.[88]

The three Philips also dragged Portugal into Spain's monetary problems. Madrid was always in desperate need of money to pay for its military involvements. Its problems were aggravated in the 1620's by a decrease in shipments of American silver. To pay its bills, Madrid levied oppressive taxes, demanded compulsory loans, and floated bonds it knew it never could redeem. It periodically debased its money and declared partial bankruptcies. The one announced by Felipe IV in 1627 was the fifth in seventy years. During this time inflation soared, food production declined, and poverty, hunger and epidemics spread. At the same time Spain was beginning to exclude the Portuguese from participation in the economic development of its Latin American colonies.

In addition, the Old Guard of Portugal faced the strongest effort yet made to subordinate it completely to the court at Madrid. At the time of the union, Spain had promised to respect Portuguese autonomy, but on more than one occasion it had taken steps to reduce it. Its efforts were not primarily motivated by hostility to the Portuguese. They corresponded to a broader plan for modernization

---

87 For this entire period, see Oliveira Marques, *History of Portugal,* 1:271–333.

88 For a summary of this period, see Martin A. Cohen, "Brazil," in Martin A. Cohen, ed., *The Jewish Experience in Latin America* (2 vols.; New York: KTAV, 1971) 1:lii–lx.

which favored the centralization of all national activities under a strong monarchy. The New Guard had been attempting to move in this direction since at least the days of the Catholic Sovereigns. Its successes were slow and regularly controlled by Spain's entrenched and resourceful Old Guard. Now, under the leadership of the Count-Duke of Olivares, the *valido* or favorite of Felipe IV, it embarked on an intensive program of administrative and financial reform, aimed at strengthening the country through centralization and rationalization. One critical goal of this program was the reduction of regional autonomy throughout the Peninsula. This hit hardest at Spain's titular partner, Portugal. Another was the creation of more efficient methods for the collection of taxes. A third was the fostering of mercantile endeavors. In the meantime, the Spanish Old Guard, led by the high aristocracy, plotted for the *valido*'s overthrow.[89]

The Portuguese New Christians figured prominently in the modernization process throughout the Peninsula. By this time the Spanish New Christians had largely disappeared while the Portuguese New Christian gained access to the rest of the Peninsula through the union with Spain.[90] Their manifold skills, particularly in the areas of administration and commerce, were indispensable to any process of modernization and efficiency. The Spanish crown and the rationalizing interests throughout the Peninsula looked with favor upon the New Christians.[91] The crown also took seriously the observation of those who pointed out that the emigrating New Christians were aiding Spain's competitors and enemies. This was especially the case after the fall of Count-Duke Olivares and the national bankruptcy in 1647. After Olivares, many leading figures in Spain even harbored the hope of enticing former New Christians back from Holland, including some who had become Jews and others who had not.[92] The seemingly

89 On the political and ideological process of the centralization of authority in the Crown, see José García Marín, *La burocracia castellana bajo los Austrias* (Seville: Universidad de Sevilla, 1976). As an example of the various forces in conflict, see its chapter "Algunos aspectos de la elección de oficios en la esfera municipal," 269–96. On the politics of the reign of Philip IV see also Antonio Domínguez Ortiz, *Política y hacienda de Felipe IV* (Madrid: Editorial de Derecho Financiero, 1960). On the Count-Duke of Olivares, in addition to the aforementioned histories of Spain and Portugal, see the classic work of Gregorio Marañón, *El Conde-Duque de Olivares* (Madrid, Espasa-Calpe, 1969) esp. chap. 7 ("La lucha contra los grandes") 74–80 and chap. 19 ("La política exterior y regional") 173–81.

90 See Lea, *History of the Inquisition*, 3:254–90.

91 See Lynch, *Spain Under the Habsbugs*, 2:140–41. See also Julio Caro Baroja, *Los judíos en la España moderna y contemporánea* (3 vols°.; Madrid: Ediciones Arion, 1962) 2:68–131.

92 A precious document in this regard is to be found in the *Colecção Pombalina*, vol. 493, no. 738, *Miscelanea: Pareceres originaes de Fr. Ricardo de S. Victor e de Fr. Dionysio dos Anjos instando para que S. M. faça o contrato de commercio com os judeus (Original Opinions of Brother Ricardo de S. Victor and Brother Dionysio dos Anjos Petitioning that Your Majesty Make a Commercial Contract with the Jews)*. See also Enrique Sasporta y Beja, "Une tentative de repatriment des Sephardim sous Philippe IV," *Le Judaisme Sephardi* 12 (1956) 549–51. For an earlier parallel initiative at the beginning of the reign of Philip III of Spain (Philip II of Portugal), see Francisco Cantera Burgos,

equivocal attitude of the crown toward the New Christians, seen especially in the reign of Felipe IV, is not to be attributed to the whim of the monarch. Rather it is to be explained as his political response to the shifting balance of power in the struggle between the constellations of the Old Guard and the New, with their conflicting agendas carefully crafted and deliberately pursued.[93]

A case in point, perhaps the best, is Felipe III's so-called "irrevocable" removal in 1605 of all restrictions against New Christian emigration. The restrictions were reimposed in 1610. In the 1620's, Felipe IV again held out the promise of unobstructed emigration. The restrictions of 1610 were lifted in 1629 and never reimposed again.[94] The role of the New Guard in the liberal gestures to the New Christians is better appreciated when it is juxtaposed to the Spanish government's consummation in the year of 1604 (!) of a commercial treaty with the heretical English. In this treaty the English were guaranteed that they would not be molested for reasons of conscience. As in the case of the New Christians, the agreements with the English evoked passionate opposition which was couched in theological terms.

Both Felipe III and Felipe IV made the New Christians pay a heavy price for their benefits: two hundred thousand cruzados in the first instance and a million and a half in the second. To attain a part of its much needed capital, the crown thus shamelessly exploited the New Christians' desire to become citizens, or, more precisely, royal subjects, on a par with everyone else, a desire which the crown and the New Guard wished to fulfill and doubtless regarded as a natural right, in conformity with the spirit of humanism pervading the liberal wing of the social spectrum. But it would be a mistake to assume that the extortion of money was all that the crown had in mind for the New Christians. The fact that most New Christians did not leave the Peninsula when the opportunity was given to them furnishes an unequivocal demonstration that they regarded the opening of its doors as a symbol of their elevation to first class citizenship and therefore to greater freedom and opportunity within the Peninsula. They

---

"El problema de los criptojudíos al escalar el trono Felipe III," *Homenaje al Profesor Alarcos García* (2 vols.; Valladolid: Univ. of Valladolid, 1965) 2:633–42. See also José Alcalá-Zamora y Queipo de Llano, *España, Flandes y el Mar del Norte (1618–39)* (Barcelona: Editorial Planeta, 1975) 250 and Daniel Maurice Swetschinski, *The Portugueuse Jewish Merchants of Seventeenth Century Amsterdam: A Social Profile* (Ann Arbor: Univ. of Michigan International, 1979) 89–95 and esp. chap. 3, "The Economic Foundations of Portuguese Jewish Life," 134–326.

93 See Henry Kamen, *Spain in the Later Seventeenth Century*, 1665–1700 (London and New York: Longman, 1980) 227.

94 Noteworthy in this regard are the words of José Antonio Maravall, ". . . There is no doubt that the increasingly hard line of the Inquisition, the measures rigorously applied against the Conversos, the expulsion of the Moriscos and the sclerosis of thought occasioned by the physical imposition of an orthodoxy are all manifestations of a retrogression in the process of political secularization," (translation mine) *La oposición política bajo los Austrias* (Esplugues de Llobregat [Barcelona]: Ediciones Ariel, 1972) 200.

flocked to the port of Seville, the capital at Madrid, and other important centers. They expanded their mercantile activities, and by the time of Olivares, obviously not without the initiative and encouragement of the court, they had assumed a significant, if not a dominant position, in the farming of the royal revenues. The revocation of the third Felipe's pledge to the New Christians is also to be explained less as a royal whim than as a royal response to the temporary supremacy of the Old Guard.

On top of all this, in Portugal, the Old Guard had by this time been effectively pushed out of the principal positions of power by a new aristocracy, resulting largely from the creation of new titles ever since its union with Spain in 1580. The creation of such titles, accelerated during the reign of Felipe IV, was intended to assure Madrid of the support of its total program. Similarly, a number of new appointments in the high strata of the Church (and the Inquisition) were made by Rome under the influence of Madrid.[95]

The unremitting erosion of its power impelled the Old Guard to desperate attempts at the marshaling of anti-New Christian sentiment. None at this time was more comprehensively characteristic than the invaluable *Treatise on the Various Means Available to His Catholic Majesty for the Remedy of Judaism in this Kingdom of Portugal* (*Tratado sobre os various meyos que se offerecerão a sua Magestade Cathólica para remedio do Judaismo neste Reyno de Portugal*). The exact date of this treatise is indeterminable, but it is justifiably estimated to have been completed around the year 1625, immediately prior to the formulation of the plans for the Assembly of Tomar. Likewise unknown is its author, though its conventional attribution to Fernão Martins Mascarenhas, who had served as Bishop of Algarve, Lisbon and Coimbra as well as Rector of the University of Coimbra and Inquisitor General of the Realm, or minimally, to Mascarenhas' circle, is most plausible.

As promised in its title, this treatise collects the remedies generally offered for dealing with Portugal's "Jewish question" or "New Christian problem." These remedies include a general pardon, a general expulsion, a partial expulsion, the exile of at least some New Christians to Portugal's colonies, and, for those in the Iberian Peninsula, the imposition of restrictions in the areas of education, occupation and residence. By the time of this treatise, the implementation of most of these remedies in their traditional articulation was beyond the reasonable hopes of even the most entrenched elements of the Old Guard. Yet, through its catalogue of time-worn remedies, generally accompanied by their respective pros and cons, this treatise appears to advocate the principled necessity for a solution to the New Christian problem and the validity of many elements in the solutions repeatedly proposed. In this way, the treatise leaves the door open for a new

95 Azevedo, *Cristãos Novos*, 155–92.

solution, based on a restructured configuration of traditional disabilities such as would effectively insure the continuation of the New Christians as a subordinate caste. Consistent with this position is the support of this treatise for the inquisitional punishment of the *dogmatistas*, the New Christians who were allegedly propagating the practice of Judaism, and its bold request that the Inquisition be given control in the determination of the purity and contamination of blood lines. The continuation of the concept of *limpeza de sangue* would keep the Marrano myth alive, and through its political utilization, the entire New Guard under inquisitional control.[96]

By the time of the Assembly of Tomar, the Portuguese Old Guard could not have failed to realize that its strength was ebbing and that a determined effort was necessary to salvage its position, or, at least, to buy time before its inevitable demise.[97] Toward this end, it moved in the two directions open to it. It galvanized anti-Spanish feeling in Portugal and a desire for independence into a revolutionary movement. And it galvanized anti-New Christian feeling into a movement for a full return to the institutions and forms of life dominant before the union.

The second effort resulted in the convocation of the Assembly of Tomar "with mature judgment and fervent zeal, to determine a means to obstruct Judaism, which has been growing to such a degree in our time and to obviate the evils which as a result we have been continually suffering." The political nature of this assembly is strongly intimated by the flimsily rationalized absence of leading Portuguese prelates from its deliberations and the failure of its supporters to secure for it the dignity of the title council (*Concílio*) instead of Assembly (*Junta*) from Rome. Felipe's permission for the convocation of the Assembly was granted, not because he had any question about the outcome of its deliberations or because he was in sympathy with its arch-conservative position, but because in his straits it was the most prudent course of action at the time. A rejection of the request would have dramatized the opposition's cause and strengthened the Portuguese Old Guard at a time of its choice and one inopportune for the court at Madrid. Granting the request temporarily channeled the opposition into a publicly scrutinizable activity and gave Madrid an opportunity to temporize by interposing numerous obstacles to the implementation of the requests carried by the Report, perhaps in the hope of burying the entire problem that had created it. All of this is patent from the facts at our disposal.

96 For a study of the Treatise, see Reuven Finegold, "The New Christian Problem in Portugal 1601–1625" (Heb.), *Zion* 54 (1989) 379–400. The author worked from a printed copy which he called a "unique copy," found in the library of the University of Coimbra. It should be noted that a copy is also to be found in the Colecção Moreira (*Colecção*), 1:70–93. Interestingly, a penciled note there reads "It is not by F. M. Mascarenhas."

97 See, e.g., the declaration, dated March 20, 1628, by Bishop João Manoel of Coimbra in *Papeis sobre a Junta de Thomar*, ANTT Cód. 1507.

At its conclusion, the Assembly delegated two of its number, the Archbishop of Evora and the Bishop of Elvas, to carry its decisions to the court in Madrid.[98] To their ostensible surprise, the two prelates tried for an entire year to secure an appointment at court before they were successful. In the interval, the Bishop of Elvas, at his request, was relieved of his responsibility and replaced by the Bishop of Coimbra, who had recently been named to the Lisbon see.[99] The Bishop of Coimbra departed for Madrid in January, 1631. In the meantime, his partner, the Archbishop of Evora, had become ill and was replaced by the Archbishop-Elect of Goa.

In the meantime, also, the New Christians had apparently become aware of the Assembly's proposals and moved to neutralize them. In a petition to the king, composed in the late spring or early summer of 1630 and containing their usual complaints against the excesses of the Inquisition, they reiterated their sincere desire to avoid heresy. They suggested that much could be accomplished toward this end if they were given periodic indoctrination into the faith under the auspices of the Inquisition.[100] Inasmuch as the same religious indoctrination had been available to them since their childhood from numerous other religious sources, this request can best be understood as an attempt by the New Christians to disarm their opponents who were using the New Christians' alleged religious deviance and incorrigibility as a rationalization for all inquisitional activity against them.

This conclusion is supported by the reaction of the members of the Junta of Tomar on learning of the New Christians' request. Instead of delighting in the New Christians' expressed desire to be guided in matters of faith, they framed a counterpetition requesting the expulsion from Portugal and its possessions of all New Christians descended from four New Christian grandparents, except if their families had shown no convictions for heresy since the general conversion of 1497. In an attempt to conceal its connection to the New Christians' request, the Doctors backdated their memorial to August 4, 1629.[101]

Further revealing the critical fissures in the position of the Old Guard was a skein of dramatic events that began a short five months after the conclusion of the Assembly of Tomar. On the night of January 15, 1630, a bunch of hoodlums forced open the sacrarium of Lisbon's St. Engracia's Church and stole the hosts prepared for mass and communion. Also in Lisbon, not long thereafter, armed men tore from the walls of various buildings a number of pious placards bearing the words "Praised be the Holy Sacrament forever," while posters laudatory of Judaism and condemnatory of Christianity appeared on major thoroughfares. In Porto Alegre a cross that had been prepared for a religious procession was

98 Report 1a and Azevedo, *Cristãos Novos*, 195 and 207.

99 Azevedo, *Cristãos Novos*, 207–8 and the *Carta do Bispo de Coimbra aos Prelados da Junta*, dated May 30, 1631, in Arquivo Nacional, Inquisição, Cód. 1508.

100 Azevedo, *Cristãos Novos*, 207.

101 Azevedo, *Cristãos Novos*, 207–8.

discovered to have been smeared with the blood of a dead dog. In Coimbra, a Franciscan friar was assassinated, while in Tomar itself an Old Christian was killed shortly after he had vowed to sign a proclamation condemning New Christians.[102] This was the first of a series of troubles for the New Christians in Coimbra, especially at the hands of student mobs and lasting several years. Finally, in Santarem and Evora, a number of crosses stabbed with knives suddenly appeared.

The New Christians were quick to impute all of these occurrences to a conspiracy of Old Christians, or in our terms, the Old Guard. For its part, the Old Guard, aided by rabble-rousing preachers and pamphleteers, placed the onus squarely on the New Christians as a group.

Except for a Majorcan accused in the death of the Franciscan friar, no one was persecuted for these crimes and no individual was named a suspect.

Aside from the enduring disturbances in Coimbra, the accusations against the New Christians spawned a two-month period of intense anti-New Christian riots by gangs of youths throughout Portugal, especially in Santarem, Torres Novos and Evora, where the university had to be closed for a while. These events emboldened the Inquisition to increase its activity.

By March 25, 1630, Archbishop João Manoel had drafted an addendum to the Report and fourteen other members of the Assembly had affixed their signatures to it. This addendum detailed the sacrileges that had occurred "since we completed the Report," and reiterated the Report's recommendation for immediate action against the New Christians. It dismissed the New Christians' defense with the allegation that the New Christians "shamelessly impute blame to those who are free of it . . . for they are children of falsehood." Regarding the New Christians they explained that "since they have the Devil within them," they are so false in their utterances that "as we can see in Holy Gospels, they gave evidence against God." The document placed the blame for all of the disturbances on the "insolence," the "ancient custom" of the New Christians as a group. Averring that with respect to Christianity the New Christians "are considered unbelievers, inconstant in the Faith, pretenders and deceivers since they place the Jewish faith in their hearts and keep the faith of Christianity only with their lips," the document determined "that the insolence of those people will never cease but rather Judaism will grow as long as they communicate with us and live in our midst." The document concludes with a new proposal. It seeks the expulsion of full New Christians; the expulsion of surviving confessed heretics and their immediate families; the expulsion of the immediate families of executed *negativos* and most of their relatives to the second degree; and some special consideration for those New Christians worthy of honors for signal service to the Republic.[103]

---

102 Theóphilo Braga, *História da Universidade de Coimbra* (4 vols.; Lisbon: Academia Real das Sciências, 1892–1902) 2:617.

103 *Proposta do Bispo de Coimbra aos Theologos da Junta de Thomar,* in ANTT, Códice 1509, no

For their part, the New Christians were aided by leading churchmen, like the Jesuit writer Diogo de Areda, who opposed a general expulsion on the ground that it would depopulate Portugal.[104] Royal counselors, both lay and clerical, also urged the abolition of all distinctions between New and Old Christians and the admittance of New Christians to important positions and honors. Foremost among these counselors was the king's confessor, Antonio de Sotomayor.

Doubtless emboldened by such protagonists, the New Christians renewed their attack against the Inquisition in a memorial addressed to Sotomayor in September of 1630. They charged that as a result of inquisitional persecution, entire towns had become depopulated and large numbers of New Christians had left the Peninsula and entered the service of Portugal's competitors. They insisted that they were good Christians and intimated that they wished another general pardon. They suggested that the responsibility for supervising their religious behavior and insuring that only true heretics would be punished should be placed upon the shoulders of the Inquisitors and "other pious and learned people."[105]

Sotomayor rejected both of the New Christians' requests. He expressed amazement at their desire to entrust their fate to the Inquisitors and suggested that the New Christians intended to suborn the Inquisitors and other pious men. At the same time he evinced a desire to find ways of encouraging New Christians to remain in Portugal and New Christian expatriates to return. He wanted to bring them all to a "true knowledge of God" by giving them security against arbitrary molestation and granting them some of the honors that were reserved for Old Christians.[106] In the meantime, The Inquisitor General, Francisco de Castro,

---

pagination. The cover page goes on to say "After the Assembly of Tomar and the Report which your Graces prepared and offered to the prelates, there occurred several events in which the people of the Nation has shown its inclinations against the Catholic faith, especially against the Most Holy Sacrament, of which events if there had been any information at that time [of the Assembly], not only would explicit mention have been made in the said Report, but, it seems, there would have been an even more urgent cause for action in matters of faith against this people than the one determined at that time and a greater obligation for arresting the damages that could be feared from their communication with the most expeditious remedies" (translation mine). Azevedo, *Cristãos Novos*, 203, n. 2, makes brief mention of João Manuel's treatise, but provides no analysis.

104 Adler, "Les Marranes d'Espagne et de Portugal," *Revue des Études Juives* 48 (1904) 16. Cf., reciprocally, Adler, "Les Marranes d'Espagne et de Portugal," *Revue des Études Juives* 49 (1904) 63 (no. 5, no date, but clearly contemporary with these events), where the New Christians exaggeratedly claim that as a result of arrests by the Inquisition, "apenas hay siudad, villa o lugar que no este despoblado."

105 Adler, "Les Marranes d'Espagne et de Portugal," *Revue des Études Juives* 50 (1905) 232.

106 Adler, "Les Marranes d'Espagne et de Portugal," *Revue des Études Juives* 50 (1905) 229–34, esp. 233. On the continuing debate over the question of blood purity during the early years of Felipe IV (Filipe III) see Henri Méchoulan, "Nouveaux Elements dans la Controverse des Statuts de Pureté de Sang en Espagne au XVII e Siècle," *Studia Rosenthaliana* 10 (1976) 142–50.

urged the expulsion of convicted Judaizers and those suspect "*de vehementi*."[107]

Throughout this struggle King Felipe hedged. On the one hand he ignored the New Christians' petitions for pardon. He ordered the selective expulsion of convicted Judaizers as suggested by the Inquisitor General and barred New Christians remaining in Portugal from important secular and religious positions and honors. On the other, he neglected to enforce these decrees and directed all future inquisitional business to come directly to the crown.[108]

If the war between the Old Guard and the New Guard appeared to be at a standstill, King Felipe's vacillation placed the advantage clearly in the New Christians' camp.

Some time after the submission of the Junta's report, the king ordered the convocation of a Junta of his own to study the Report and deal with "the details of the people of the Nation of the Kingdom of Portugal." He transmitted the order to his confessor, Sotomayor, in a memorandum dated March 26, 1631.[109] At the king's request, Sotomayor recommended an Inquisitor and a theologian to serve on the commission. The Inquisitor was Juan Mendes (Méndez) de Tavora, delegate of the Lisbon Inquisition, who also bore the honorific title of "Vicegroom of the King's Bedchamber" (*sumiller de cortina*). The theologian was Manuel de Vega (Veiga) Cabral. The identity and numbers of the rest of the commission are not known.

Their analysis of the Report led this Junta to deduce fourteen questions or propositions which were to form the basis for their reaction. The fourteen points were as follows:

1. That it was permissible to expel all Jews and all people with a drop of Jewish blood in their veins;

2. That the expulsion could be limited to those who could not be expected to convert sincerely and who were the leaders of Judaism;

3. That the king, as a sovereign lord, had the right to expel New Christians of pure Jewish blood and confiscate their possessions, except those with a long family tree never stigmatized by any Judaizing;

4. That the Church should be the sole judge in these matters, since the offense was directed against the faith;

---

107 Adler, "Les Marranes d'Espagne et de Portugal," *Revue des Études Juives* 49 (1904) 67–72, esp. 67 and 71.

108 Azevedo, *Cristãos Novos*, 211–21.

109 Adler, "Les Marranes d'Espagne et de Portugal," *Revue des Études Juives* 50 (1905) 236–37. See also 51 (1906) 97–120 and 251–64.

5. That Old Christian spouses and children of penitents reconciled for Judaism should not be exiled;

6. That the expulsion should be at the discretion of the Inquisitors, who might therefore choose not to apply this penalty;

7. That the penalty of exile be applicable to New Christian spouses (having at least one New Christian grandparent) of New Christians reconciled to the Church after having foresworn the crimes of which they were suspect, or, as the Inquisition's official jargon described it, after having abjured *de vehementi*;

8. That the penalty of exile be applicable to New Christian spouses and children of Judaizers condemned to the stake;

9. That no other penance or punishment which may have been given and ful-filled in part or totally should exempt such people from exile;

10. That the king should order the expulsion of all remaining New Christians (not subject to exile in any of the above categories) within the period of a year, permitting them to sell their possessions, but not to take jewelry, gold or silver out of the country, and warning them that anyone returning to the country would be condemned to the galleys;

11. That to arrest the prejudicial propagation of Judaism caused by the mar-riages of New Christians to Old Christians the king should limit the dowries that New Christians provide for such marriages, and disqualify the Old Christian partners from court privileges, honors and public positions;

12. That the king should ask the pope, "in order to avoid sacrilege, to declare that all New Christians, even to the tenth generation, be prohibited from church dignities and canonries in metropolitan, cathedral and collegial churches, and from all other ecclesiastical benefits, even the obtaining of minor orders";

13. That the king declare the New Christians incapable of receiving secular dignities or positions; and

14. That the New Christians be excluded from all contact and business with the Old Christians.

With a scholarly thoroughness rivaling that of the Tomar report, the royal com-mission proceeded to explode the foundations of the Marrano myth and reject each of the propositions. In its opinion, submitted by Sotomayor, it makes an unmistakable distinction between New Christians and Jews. It denies any inherent hostility to Christianity by the descendants of the forced converts of 1497. It cites the large number of New Christian clergy and the New Christians' pious support of the principles and institutions of the Church as proof of their continued devotion to Catholicism. It even asserts that the original converts themselves became good Christians. It insists that if the New Christians are somewhat suspect because of their "blood," this does not make them deserving of expulsion.

A general expulsion of the New Christians would be unjust, the king's commission states. The New Christians should not be regarded as a cohesive group [sic!]. They have never constituted themselves as such and the Church has never created such sub-communities by segregating Christian from Christian [sic!]. A general expulsion would involve the innocent as well as the guilty. The expulsion of New Christians on the ground that their ancestors had been suspect in matters of faith would involve punishment for someone else's guilt and as such would contradict canon law. The same reasoning militates against the expulsion of spouses and children of condemned Judaizers. Such a policy, unprecedented in Christian tradition, would in fact violate the fundamental right of all Christians to repent their sins and be reconciled to the Church. As everywhere else, the Iberian Church has always practiced kindness rather than rigor with sinners. "The Church opens the doors of its mercy to those whom it reconciles to its bosom, and when it does so, it prudently presumes that they are deserving of such mercy," the commission says. "How then can it be just and reasonable," they ask "that . . . it is condemning them to perpetual exile when it should be . . . admitting them to union and fellowship?" The commission expresses doubt regarding the Inquisition that "the beneficent power which Christ our Lord communicated to it for upbuilding and not for destruction (*in aedificationem, non in destructionem*) could properly be extended to the expulsion of so many people under the conditions and circumstances proposed." Not incidentally, the commission points out that a general expulsion is not even politically justified, as it was in the case of the *moriscos*.

A limited expulsion is also undesirable, the commission states. It would not satisfy the Portuguese clerics who insist that the entire nation is contaminated with New Christian blood, and its disruption of families would damage the entire nation.

The commission's clerics and other scholars concede that the king has the right to expel New Christians, but at the same time they emphasize his responsibility to do what is right and serve his nation best.

The penalty of exile should not be left to the discretion of the Church or the Inquisition, they believe, because, in contradiction of religious principle, this could only lead to arbitrariness.

They oppose the expulsion of confessors *de vehementi* on the ground of the double punishment, that is, the normal penance and exile, to which they would thereby be exposed.

They forcefully reject the expulsion of the New Christian residue mentioned in proposition 10. Such expulsion, they explain, adopting the general New Guard vocabulary of the modern world, would deprive these New Christians of "the natural liberty in which they were born." It would also be politically counterproductive. The New Christians constitute a considerable proportion of Portuguese society, they emphasize. They cannot be expelled without dismembering the state. It would be just as corrosive to prevent New Christians from leaving the country. Such a policy would be "foreign to every Christian government and destined to create uprising, tumults and unrest, which always come from oppressed spirits." Emphasizing that "it is not possible to put doors on a kingdom," the commission urges that the New Christians be given the full right of coming and going and the right to sell their property if they should decide to leave.

Sotomayor and his colleagues oppose all restrictions against marriages between New Christians and Old Christians. The government may control the life and death of its subjects, they say, but it does not possess the right to interfere with the licit propagation of the human race. Besides, no one is compelling Old Christians to marry New Christians, they point out. Additionally, such interference would, in opposition to the policy of the Church, involve the crown in the creation of an impediment to marriage. Only the Pope can do this. The practice would also lead to the further stigmatization of citizens and all kinds of strife. Far from preventing them, the king, they say, should encourage such unions "because of our insufficiency of people for commerce and conquests."

Similarly, Sotomayor and his colleagues reject all impediments to the religious and secular preferment of New Christians and oppose the exclusion of New Christians from business contact with Old Christians. They emphasize the need for national leadership to develop the talents and strengthen the unity of its people. The complete assimilation of the New Christians would be attained by the policy they suggest rather than the current policy of repression and separation.[110] The royal commission's rejection of the Marrano myth revealed the turning of the tables of power in Portugal in favor of its New Guard.

The revolutionary movement itself proved disastrous to the Old Guard, even though its revolt against Spain led to the restoration of Portuguese independence in 1640. The problem of the Old Guard was partially due to the divisions within the Old Guard itself. Many elements of the Old Guard had not favored the revolt. Contributing even more to the decline of the Old Guard was the

110 Adler, "Les Marranes d'Espagne et de Portugal," *Revue des Études Juives* 51 (1906) 98–115: document dated 25 March 1631 ("Junta tocante a los de la nación de Portugal diferente de la del Obispo de Coimbra") and 115–20 and 251–58, "Parecer del Confesor," dated January 1, 1633.

participation in the revolt of significant groups of New Christian merchants, among them many with international ties, particularly to Portugal's primary colony in Brazil.

Even more deleterious to the interests of the Old Guard were the decades of instability suffered by Portugal after the severance of its ties with Spain. Until 1668, Spain refused to recognize Portugal's independence and fought to restore it to its control. In the meantime, Portugal suffered continual attacks against its holdings in the Indian Ocean and lost Muscat, its last bastion in the Persian Gulf. Only on its Atlantic front was it able to hold its position, as it moved to oust the Dutch from Brazil. Portugal's situation did not begin to stabilize until it entered into a dual union with England in the form of a commercial treaty in 1654 and the marriage in 1662 of England's Charles II with Dona Catarina, daughter of Portugal's João IV (1640–56). The English connection proved to be one of the most important factors in Portugal's survival as an independent nation.

In 1641, members of Portugal's high aristocracy, the high clergy and elements of the merchant class with business interests in Spain and its colonies, staged an abortive revolt against João IV. Less dramatic struggles continued into the reign of the mentally deficient Afonso VI (1656–67) and the early years of the monarchy of Pedro II (1667–1706).[111]

Corresponding to the instability was the recrudescence of inquisitional activity against the New Christians during the reign of João IV, Afonso VI and the early years of Pedro II. The peak periods of this activity came in the years 1649–57, with over six hundred condemnations for Judaism in two autos-da-fé in Evora alone and 1662–67, when nearly sixteen hundred were sentenced. All but a handful of these convicts, it should be pointed out, were reconciled to the Church. Considerably less than two percent were sent to the stake.

Accompanying the arrests and trials of these victims of the Inquisition were much publicized charges of host desecration, thefts of church vessels, and other worn and wooden canards.[112]

These were valetudinarian efforts. The New Guard was gaining power and the monarchy knew where its interests lay. Numerous and influential leaders, prominent among them the eloquent Jesuit António Vieira, the "Apostle of Brazil," urged such policies as the ingathering of exiled New Christians and the abolition of all the disabilities of the New Christian class.[113] As João IV accepted such

---

111 See Oliveira Marques, *History of Portugal*, 1:330 and, for a broader view of this period, 322–94. See also Livermore, *A New History of Portugal*, 173–204. On this period see Carl A. Hanson, *Economy and Society in Baroque Portugal 1668–1703* (Minneapolis: Univ. of Minnesota Press, 1981), which, however, regards the "converso problem" from an essentially religious perspective. See esp. chap. 4, "The New Christian Challenge to the Established Order," 75–107.

112 Azevedo, *Cristãos Novos*, chap. 6 to 8, 236–330.

113 See his writings on the "Jews and the Inquisition," in Vieira, *Obras Escolhidas*. On Vieira, see the still indispensable work of João Lúcio Azevedo, *História de António Vieira* (2 vols.; Lisbon: A.M.

counsel, he weaned himself from the Old Guard and displayed impatience if not hostility toward the Inquisition.

In 1674, less than two decades after João's death, Pope Clement X suspended the Inquisition and five years later the Inquisitors themselves. The Inquisitors were, however, restored in 1681.[114]

In the eighteenth century, the Portuguese Inquisition flexed its muscles in small but frightening regional holocausts. But when Sebastião José de Carvalho y Mello, later the Marquis of Pombal (1699–1782), and Prime Minister of Portugal (1756–82) first attained power in 1751, he forbade the celebration of autos-da-fé without the permission of the civil authorities. Seventeen years later he ordered the destruction of all registers designating Portuguese families as New Christians. On May 23, 1773, he abolished all legal distinctions between New Christians and Old Christians and even ordered families claiming pure Old Christian blood to intermarry with New Christians within a four month period.[115]

Teixeira, 1918, 1920). See also Azevedo, *Cristãos Novos*, 243–46. and 284–88. And Israel Salvator Révah, "Les Jesuites portugais contre l'Inquisition," *Revista do livro* 1 (December 1956) nos. 3-4, 29–53. On the imputation of unclean blood to Vieira see again António Baião, "O sangue infecto do Pe. António Vieira," *O Instituto* 77 (1929) 1–10. For a succinct summary of Vieira's activities, see Elias Lipiner, *Izaque de Castro: O mancebo que veio preso do Brasil*(Recife: Fundação Joaquim Nabuco, Editora Massangana,1992) 271–72.

114 Azevedo, *Cristãos Novos*, 310–22. In addition to the general works on the Inquisition mentioned above in n. 75 see now also, inter alia, António Borges Coelho, *Inquisição de Evora. Dos primórdios a 1668* (2 vols.; Lisbon: Caminho,1987); and Sara T. Nalle, *God in La Mancha: Religious Reform and the People of Cuenca, 1500–1650* (Baltimore: Johns Hopkins Univ. Press,1992). For some interesting insights on the state of religion on the Spanish side of the border see Alvaro Huerga,"Exaltación y crisis de la religiosidad española en el siglo XVII" *História e filosofia* 1 (Lisbon, 1982) 239–58, esp. 241. For parallels in Latin America, see the standard works by José Toribio Medina, *Historia del tribunal del Santo Oficio de la Inquisición en México* ([Santiago de Chile: Imprenta Elzeviriana,1905] San Angel, Mexico: Consejo Nacional para la Cultura y las Artes,1991); *Historia del tribunal de la Inquisición de Lima, (1569-1820)* (2 vols.; [Santiago de Chile: Impena Gutenberg,1887] Santiago de Chile: Fondo histórico y bibliográfico J. T. Medina, 1956); *Historia del tribunal del Santo Oficio de la Inquisición de Cartagena de las Indias* ([Santiago de Chile: Imprenta Elzeviriana,1899] Bogota: C.Valencia, 1978); *Historia del tribunal del Santo Oficio en Chile* (Santiago de Chile: Imprenta Ercilla, 1890); *El tribunal del Santo Oficio de la Inquisición en las provincias del Plata* (Santiago de Chile: Imprenta Elzeviriana, 1899); and more recently, Paulino Castanedo Delgado and Pilar Hernández Aparicio and (for vol. 3) René Millar Carvacho, *La Inquisición de Lima (1570–1635)* (3 vols.; Madrid: Editorial Deimos,1989–98); as well as two works by Solange Alberro, *La actividad del Santo Oficio de la Inquisición en Nueva España 1571–1700* (Mexico: Instituto Nacional de Antropología e Historia, Departamento de Investigaciones Históricas, Seminario de Histria de las Mentalidades y Religión en el México Colonial,1981) and *Inquisition et société en Mexique 1571–1700* (Mexico City: Centre d'etudes mexicaines et centramericaines,1988).

115 On the Portuguese Inquisition in the early eighteenth century see Teresa Pinto Leite, *Inquisição e Cristãos Novos no reinado de João V [1707-50]: Alguns aspectos de história social* (Lisbon: Faculdade de Letras,1962). On Pombal, see Raul Rêgo, *O Marquês de Pombal, os cristãos-novos e a Inquisição* (Lisbon, 1984)347 ff. See also Francisco José Calazans Falcón, *A época Pombalina (Política Econó-mica e Monarquia Ilustrada)* (São Paolo: Editora Atica, 1982) esp. 160–79 and 377–445. On the

Despite Pombal's transformations, Portugal remained a Catholic country. The concessions to the New Christians and restrictions on the Inquisition did not result in an upsurge of Jewish practice or identification with Judaism, however broadly such practice or identification may be defined. On the contrary, the New Christians for the most part were quickly and fully assimilated into the general Portuguese population.[116]

The claim of the New Christians and their Old Christian supporters, never more cogently made than at the time of the Assembly of Tomar, that precisely this would happen, thus proved to be correct. Unfortunately the failure of Portugal as a total society to accept their point of view in time prevented it from capitalizing on its early advantages in the fields of exploration and colonization. The ponderous weight of the Old Guard forces, acting in their own self-interest, kept Portugal from remaining the frontline, pioneering power that it once was and appeared long destined to be.

The fate of the visible New Christians in seventeenth century Spain, most of them immigrants or descendants of immigrants from Portugal, followed a parallel course. The policies of Olivares seem clearly to be headed toward the removal of the distinctions between Old Christians and New Christians. During his incumbency, the New Christians actually petitioned for a removal of their disabilities in Spain. In 1634, Olivares began negotiations with Jews in the Middle East and North Africa which would have permitted at least some to reside in Spain and even to create a synagogue of their own. Olivares was also believed to be contemplating the abolition of the Inquisition.

Olivares' forced resignation in 1643 and the forced exile in 1669 of the Jesuit Johann Nithard, confessor and advisor to the Queen during the minority of Carlos II (1665–75), turned out to provide only short-lived victories for Spain's Old Guard. A plethora of problems, including revolts in Sicily and Naples and at home in Catalonia, churned up a manifold discontent that kept Spain's political system unstable.[117]

---

tenacity of the old nobility in the eighteenth century Spain and the belletristic critiques of the ennoblement of members of the New Guard see Antonio Domínguez Ortiz, *Sociedad y estado en el siglo XVIII español* (Barcelona: Ariel, 1976) 345–58.

116 See Herman Prins Salomon, "New Light on the Portuguese Inquisition: The Second Reply to the Archbishop of Cranganor," *Studia Rosenthaliano* 5:2 (July, 1971) 178–86, esp. 184. See also Salomon, *Portrait of a New Christian: Fernão Alvares Melo (1569–1632)* (Paris: Fundação Calouste Gulbenkian, Centro Cultural Português, 1982) 172, on the tenacity of the Inquisition, between the Assembly of Tomar and the advent of Pombal, in opposing even a limited expulsion of its surviving victims.

117 See, for example, Payne, *A History of Spain and Portugal*, 1:308–21 and, among the single-volume histories, Rhea Marsh Smith, *Spain: A Modern History* (Ann Arbor: University of Michigan, 1965) 194–97. The fate of the New Christians in Spain lies beyond the scope of this study and is presented here in outline form for closure only. A fuller treatment will be found in my essay in *The Sephardim in the Americas*. It should be stated that it is by no means fortuitous that the gradual decline of the Inquisition in the eighteenth century was accompanied by unmistakable social changes in the

The fall of Olivares and the depression following the government's bankruptcy in 1647 resulted in the flight of many of Spain's New Christians from the Peninsula and the deterioration of the position of those who remained.[118] The Inquisition intensified its activity during this period and renewed its intensity in the third and early part of the fourth decades of the eighteenth century. By this time the Bourbons were on the Spanish throne. Their policies favored the Enlightenment, the New Guard, and the rationalization of government. Significantly, the Inquisition's renewed activity followed by only a few years the first full centralization of government in Spain since the time of the Romans.[119] This centralization put an end, at least symbolically, to the societal control of the old Spanish grandees.[120]

From that time on, persecutions for the alleged practice of Judaism diminished. In the last forty years of the Inquisition in Spain, from 1780 until its suppression in 1820, only sixteen people were tried for Judaism. Of these, ten were foreign Jews illegally present in the Peninsula. The Inquisition was formally abolished in 1834.[121]

In retrospect, the Assembly of Tomar looms as the last colossal clash between the Portuguese Old and New Guards before the tide of battle turned. The Report of the Assembly of Tomar represents the last major articulation of the platform of the Old Guard forces behind the Inquisition.

The value of Report of the Assembly of Tomar cannot be overstated. In their presentation of the "Marrano Myth," the Doctors at the Assembly of Tomar were

---

direction of increasing the middle classes, and, in general, the New Guard. See, for example, Antonio Domínguez Ortiz, *La sociedad española en el siglo XVIII* (Madrid: Instituto Balmes de Sociología, Departamento de Historia Social, Consejo Superior de Investigaciones Científicas, 1955) 23. See also Ortiz, *Sociedad y estado en el siglo XVIII español*, esp. 279–515. On the economic implications of these changes see Juan. Plaza Prieto, *Estructura económica de España en el siglo XVIII* (Madrid: Confederación española de Cajas de Ahorros, 1976) esp. 341ff.

118 See n. 92 above.

119 On the Inquisition in the eighteenth century, in addition to the general works mentioned in nn. 115 and 116 above, see also Antonio Alvarez de Morales, *Inquisición e Ilustración (1700–1834)* (Madrid: Fundación Univ. Española, 1982) and Richard Herr, *The Eighteenth Century Revolution in Spain 1700–1834* (Princeton: Princeton Univ. Press, 1958) 201–336.

120 As precisely stated by Ortiz, *Sociedad y estado en el siglo XVIII español*, 354: "La novedad consistía en que ahora hasta los nobles de más rancia alcurnia comprendían la necesidad de fundamentar la nobleza en razones que no derivasen de la herencia biológica."

121 Lea, *History of the Inquisition*, 4:385–471 and, for pertinent documents, 541–6. For a deeper and up-to-date study of the Inquisition in the century leading to its abolition, see now Francisco. Martí Gilabert, *La abolición de la Inquisición en España* (Pamplona: Ediciones Univ. de Navarra, Univ. de Navarra, 1975). An example of the continuing function of the Inquisition as a mechanism for control of suspect thought and individuals is to be found in inquisitional attempts to control the library of the Royal Institute of Navigation and Mineralogy, founded at Gijón, Spain by the humanist Melchor de Jovellanos, one of whose patrons was himself an inquisitor at Barcelona. See Lucienne Domergue, *Les Démêlés de Jovellanos avec l'Inquisition* (Oviedo: Cátedra Feijóo, Facultad de Filosofía y Letras, Univ. de Oviedo, 1971) esp. 14 ff.

able to draw on the two centuries of its development. The Report contains the most comprehensive and detailed presentation of the myth found anywhere in the literature. The Doctors studied their sources with a dogged thoroughness and extracted from it the concepts and examples they deemed most appropriate for their case.

Perhaps better than any other single source, the Report of the Assembly of Tomar exposes the fragility of the traditional simplistic and monolithic presentation of the relationship between the Inquisition and the New Christians. In its light, responsible scholarship can no longer regard this relationship as revolving exclusively or even primarily around an axis of religion. On the contrary, it is apparent that the religious factor, important as it was, constituted only one of the manifold dimensions of this relationship. A systematic analysis and holistic reconstruction of all these dimensions reveals the history of the New Christians to be not an aberrant, tangential eddy in the mainstream of Iberian life, but one of the powerful central currents that affected the very fiber of its being.

An analysis of the Report of the Assembly of Tomar ineluctably calls for a detailed elucidation of this theme. It calls for a reevaluation of all the basic evidence on the Inquisition and the New Christians against the background of the total society in which their history transpired. Such work requires more than a knowledge of Judaism and Catholicism and a passion for or against the New Christians. It entails the application of the latest techniques of the disciplines developed to understand society. These include history, sociology, economics, politics, social psychology, and their interplay with literatures, philosophies, ideologies and ideals. The measured application of the knowledge provided by these disciplines to the myriad of known facts repeatedly rehashed in the past bids fair to produce new insights in the history not only of the New Christians, but also of the Western European countries and colonies in which they played a seminal role.

Epilogue

The struggle in Portugal climaxed by the Assembly of Tomar was part of a larger confrontation between Old Guard and New Guard constellations throughout Europe as it moved into the modern world. Because of different sociopolitical contexts and historical circumstances, this confrontation, though recognizable throughout, assumed a distinctive form in every land. Yet throughout Europe, even if in different degrees, we can trace the efforts of pre-modern elements, clerical as well as lay, to control the process and therefore the prerogatives of modernization. In every case, though again to different degrees in different lands and different times, the strategy of control required the elevation to Old Guard status of some parvenus who had been catapulted into prominence by the success of their New Guard activities. Such action by the Old Guard, or more precisely, the controlling factions of the Old Guard, inevitably involved struggle within the Old

Guard. At the same time it tacitly signaled a recognition of the indispensability of the New Guard while at the same time reminding it of which coalition was determined to remain in ultimate control.[122]

In all European countries, with the possible exception of the Soviet Union, this strategy has provided for the perpetuation to significant degrees of pre-modern institutions, standards and elements of power. The exposition of the relationship between the Iberian Peninsula and the rest of Europe in this regard requires a study far beyond the scope of this essay.

122 On this subject see, e.g., Arno J. Mayer, *The Persistence of the Old Regime: Europe to the Great War* (New York: Pantheon Books, 1981).